The
Native American
Sweat Lodge

Other books by Joseph Bruchac

Dawn Land, a novel

Return of the Sun
Native American Tales from the Northeast Woodlands

Iroquois Stories
Heroes and Heroines, Monsters and Magic

Hoop Snakes, Hide Behinds & Side-Hill Winders
Adirondack Tall Tales

Keepers of the Earth
Native American Stories and Environmental Activities for Children

Keepers of the Animals
Native American Stories and Wildlife Activities for Children

THE
NATIVE AMERICAN
SWEAT LODGE

HISTORY AND LEGENDS

BY
JOSEPH BRUCHAC

The Crossing Press, Freedom, CA 95019

Library of Congress Cataloging-in-Publication Data

Bruchac, Joseph, 1942-
    The native American sweat lodge : history & legends / by Joseph
Bruchac.
        p. cm.
    Includes bibliographical references.
    ISBN 0-89594-637-8 (cloth). -- ISBN 0-89594-636-X (paper)
        1. Indians of North America--Sweatbaths. 2. Indians of North
America--Legends. I. Title.
E98.S94B78 1993
391'.64--dc20
                                        93-5280
                                        CIP

CONTENTS

THE SWEAT LODGE

The Sweat Lodge

The sweat lodge is one of the most widespread traditions in Native North America. The first Europeans who described it were the Spanish. They observed what they called the *temezcalli* among the native peoples of Mexico. (*Teme* is the word in the Aztec language, Nahuatl, for "to bathe." *Calli* is the word in Nahuatl for "house.") It was such a strange and seemingly unhealthy custom to the various Spanish missionaries who followed the conquistadors that they spent almost as much time describing the temescal as they did trying to eradicate it.

One variety or another of the sweat lodge is found virtually everywhere in North America. In the northeast, lodges framed of willow poles might be covered with birch bark or skins. In the southeast, sweat lodges might be in earth mounds or dug into the side of a hill by a stream. On the plains, the lodge was covered with buffalo skins, while in California the sweat house was both dwelling place and ceremonial center. In the far northwest, sweat houses were sometimes made of cedar planks and even the polar Inuit engaged in sweats in their iglus.

The most widespread sweat lodge tradition today is that of the Lakota Sioux, who call it *inipi*. The Lakota people were tenacious in clinging to the inipi through a time when many other American Indian tribes were forced by the pressure of the missionaries and the Federal government to give up their sweat lodges. In some Indian communities generations passed by without sweats being held because of this pressure from church and civil authorities. The old men and women who knew how to do the sweat lodge died without passing on their knowledge to the next generation. In the last three decades, many Lakota elders have shown great generosity in sharing their sacred ceremonies with other Native communities that have wished to reinstate the sweat lodge. They have also shared with individual Indians who grew up in urban areas outside of the reservations. The inipi sweat lodge has even been brought by spiritual elders into

2

maximum security prisons for the benefit of Indian inmates. For the American Indian Movement, formed in 1968, the inipi sweat lodge became a spiritual base for a growing political awareness.

My own first experience in a sweat lodge was a very special one. I had heard and read about sweat lodges for many years and I understood that they had been, until recently, a part of Abenaki traditions. (At Mississquoi, the Abenaki community in northern Vermont, sweat baths were still taking place fairly regularly fifty years ago, but the use of sweats among most of the Native peoples of New York and New England had become a rarity by the 1960s.) I had reached a time in my life when I felt the need to engage in sweats, but I was sensitive about intruding upon other people's traditional ways. None of the Abenaki elders who were my teachers then had direct knowledge about the sweat lodge. So I asked Swift Eagle, an elderly Pueblo/Apache friend of mine, what I might do to learn about the sweat lodge. "If you really need something," he said, "be prepared. Then it will come to you."

The next day, I got a phone call from an Iroquois friend. A group of two hundred Native people were heading our way in a run from Buffalo to New York City in support of indigenous rights and Leonard Peltier. They needed a place to spend a night. Did we have room? When the group arrived and set up their camp in the backyards of our house and the house of my sister, they made themselves so comfortable that the one night turned into three days. Lakotas, Iroquois, Ojibways and other native men, women, and children of more than twenty different tribal nations were everywhere. The sound of the drum and forty-niner songs reverberated from the little house out back where my great-grandparents spent their final years. The kitchen was piled high with boxes of fry bread, and the bathtub was filled with sweetgrass being soaked. On the second day, Leonard Crow Dog, the Lakota medicine man who has been a spiritual advisor for AIM from its inception, decided that it would be right for them to do a sweat. My father told them they could build a lodge on Bell

Brook in the woods behind his house. He gave them his blessing and a deer antler to help move the heated stones. My two young sons and I were invited to help out and then invited into the lodge. Before Crow Dog left, he gave the lodge to our family and instructed us in how to use it to help ourselves and our relations.

As a result of their commitment to sharing their traditions, a number of Lakota and non-Lakota Natives (who have been trained by Lakota teachers) travel around the continent offering the inipi to their own people and, sometimes, to non-Indians. Today, it seems that wherever Indian people are found in Canada and the United States, sweat lodges are being used. Unfortunately, non-Indian and Indian "medicine men" and self-styled shamans can also be found offering sweat lodges (sometimes for a fee which may be as high as $500 a head!) not only in North America, but even in Europe. Tipis and inipis can be found each year along the Rhine. It has reached a point where one publication, *The European Journal of Native Studies,* now has a regular feature called "the plastic medicine man watch." This exposes some of the phonies who bilk unsuspecting Europeans (some of whom are ordinary working-class people with little money) out of large sums to take part in "sacred sweats."

The practice of pouring water over heated stones to produce a cleansing steam bath is common, of course, in many parts of the world and is not a practice limited to the indigenous people of the American continents. Had the first Europeans to visit Mexico not been Spaniards but Scandinavians, they would have felt much more at home with the temescal. The *savusauna* or sauna of Finland is much like the Indian sweat; I have been told by Scandinavian friends that it, too, has its roots in ceremony. Mikkel Aaland, in his world-spanning study of steam bathing traditions, *Sweat,* records an old saying from Finland: "In the sauna one must conduct himself as one would in church." Many Scandinavians still feel that the cleansing which it gives them is, like a sweat lodge, not just of the body, but of the mind and the soul. Cleansing in itself, of course, is commonly seen as a sacra-

Sweat lodge of the type used on the Plateau

mental act in many cultures. But among the Native people of North America, the sweat lodge is more sacrament than recreation. It is strongly associated with prayer and preparation.

If sweat lodges are becoming more common now, perhaps it is only returning to the way it was before European domination and the official disapproval of the United States government. These made the sweat lodge much less common in the period between the 1930s and the 1960s. I have been told by elderly Native people in many communities that they remember times in their youth when there was a sweat lodge in everyone's back yard and people would do sweats as often as once a day. Clearly, the sweat lodge can be a communal experience or an intensely personal one.

I have been directly involved in building sweat lodges and taking part in sweats for over a decade. Because of all the things which taking part in this tradition has given me, I speak of the sweat lodge with the deepest respect. That respect led me to write this book—not as a how-to or a spiritual guide, but as a way of expressing my thanks and respect.

I have seen continuing interest and involvement in sweats and other traditional Native "religious" practices among non-Natives. The growing men's movement has now embraced the sweat lodge. Sometimes enthusiasm has far outstripped the knowledge and ability of the non-Native people who involve themselves in and even lead these ceremonies. Much of what I have seen and read of non-Native practices associated with "sweats" fills me with misgivings. I would like to help set the record straight. People need to realize that involvement in a sweat lodge, not to mention leading a sweat, is not something to be taken lightly.

If you lead a sweat, you are responsible for the safety of everyone in the lodge with you. If you enter the sweat lodge, you should do so with a clear mind; if you have troubles when you enter the lodge, you cannot hide them in your heart. You can pray for cleansing, but if you are not ready to be cleansed of such things as anger and jealousy, you would be better off not entering at all. Your physical health is also a consideration. It is the responsibility of the leader of a sweat to know if anyone is suffering from some physical ailment—heart disease, perhaps, or emphysema, which might be made worse by the conditions inside a sweat lodge. I know of several occasions in the last few years when people have died in sweat lodges. It is not a common thing that someone should be harmed by a sweat. You are in more physical danger crossing the street in New York City than crawling into a sweat lodge. However, crossing a street or entering a lodge, one must know what to look out for. When someone inside the lodge says that he or she cannot stand it any longer, the one running the sweat listens to what is said.

One purpose of this book, then, is to explain something of the history, the meaning, and the use of the sweat lodge as it was and still is being practiced by Native people. Through the retelling of traditional tales in which the sweat lodge has a central place, describing building and using a sweat lodge drawn from my own personal experience, and quoting from other Native (and some non-Native) participants in sweats, I hope to lead the reader towards the beginning of a broad understanding.

It should be noted that the stories in this book are from a number of different Native cultures throughout North America. Even some American Indian people today sometimes think that there is only one way to do a sweat—the way they have been taught within their culture or (if their own original sweat lodge traditions have been set aside) within a Lakota-style inipi. Yet, as the historical survey which follows this introduction will illustrate, there are not only many varieties of the inipi-type sweats, there are at least three major types of sweat structures: the lodge into which stones are brought in and water is poured on them; the lodge in which no water is used and the central fire is made in the lodge (which is often used as a dwelling place as well as for sweats), and the Mayan and Aztec method of using a duct to convey the heat from a fire into a stone or clay sweat house. I hope that reading these stories will help both Native and non-Native people see more clearly the central and specific roles which the various kinds of sweat lodges have played and continue to play in many Native nations.

The book also includes discussion of the ways in which sweat lodges are being presented and used by people in the men's movement and by certain non-Indian, Indian, and purportedly Indian teachers who offer sweats to the general public for a fee. I am deeply opposed to the commercialization of Native religious practices.

On the other hand, there is a long-standing American Indian tradition of giving gifts to a medicine person or to someone whom you ask to help you with a healing sweat. Medicine people have to eat, too, and one should not mistake reciprocation and mutual support for commercialism. Unfortunately, in a capitalistic culture many people get the idea that anything and everything is for sale. There is no price tag on a truly traditional sweat and, unlike a labeled item on a shelf, just having the money to pay for it does not give someone the right to have it.

I want to emphasize that I am neither an expert nor a religious teacher, just a storyteller who likes to hear a tale told the right way. However, I am as capable of mistakes as anyone. If there are errors in this book, I apologize for them and I hope that those who know more than I know will help me to correct them. I am no more than a human being. When I enter the sweat lodge, I do so on my knees, close to the Mother of us all, this Earth.

HISTORICAL SURVEY

Historical Survey

Why sweat? It has long been known in many parts of the world that sweating is often therapeutic and, in many cases, healing. "Give me a fever and I can cure any disease." So said Hippocrates. Although I am not equipped to fully discuss the medical benefits of sweating, here are some interesting facts I have gleaned from a number of sources.

First of all, sweating is a very necessary bodily function. It removes toxins so effectively that the skin has been called "the third kidney." If the skin and the sweat passages are completely clogged, a human being will die within a matter of hours.

Secondly, a great many viral agents and bacteria cannot survive at temperatures much higher than 98.6° Fahrenheit. When we sweat, we literally burn away some illnesses.

Thirdly, many of the important endocrine glands are stimulated by an inner rise in temperature. Impurities in many body organs are flushed out as the capillaries dilate and the heart increases its pace to keep up with the demands for blood. (Finnish studies indicate that this does not cause a rise in blood pressure. In fact, people with high blood pressure experience a marked, though temporary reduction in their blood pressure when sweating in a sauna.)

Fourth, in a sweat bath where rocks are heated and water is poured onto them, an abundance of negative ions is released into the air. Negative ions counter fatigue and tenseness. An excess of positive ions (a condition often found in smoggy areas and in houses with central air conditioning) has been linked to asthma, heart attacks, insomnia and allergies, among other ailments.

The Basic Types of Sweats

Two basic types of sweat baths were in common use in North America at the time of the coming of the first Europeans. The vapor-bath sweat involves heating stones in a fire outside the lodge. The stones are carried inside, the lodge is sealed, and after cedar and sweetgrass are placed on the stones, water is poured to create steam. When the sweat is concluded, the participants leave the sweat lodge. Usually the coverings are then removed from the lodge to cleanse it before another sweat takes place. The direct-fire sweat is most commonly found in parts of the Arctic, among some of the Inuit, and in California. (Other Inuit groups, however, make use of the steam-bath form of the lodge by heating the stones inside a small dome-shaped structure of bent poles covered by skins and blankets, removing the remaining burning coals from them, and then pouring on the water.)

Among most of the Native peoples of California, the sweat house is a permanent structure in which fires are built to create a dry heat which causes those in the house to sweat. The heat can be almost as intense as in the vapor bath, but unlike the sweat lodge used in the vapor bath, participants in the direct-fire sweat may live full-time in the sweat house or make use of it as a ceremonial center on a continuing basis. Among the Inuit, respirators made of fibers were often used during sweats to prevent the burning of the throats and lungs of the participants.

The temescal of the Native peoples of Mexico appears to be in some ways a combination of these first two. The temescal or, as the Mayan people call it, the *zampul-che*, is a permanent structure. In the great temples of the Aztecs and Mayan, they were made of stone and lined with tiles. Today, in villages all over southern and eastern Mexico and Guatemala, the temescals are made of stone or adobe bricks. The fire for the temescal is built in an oven which is adjacent to the sweating chamber, sharing a wall with it and sometimes with a heating duct to conduct the fire's heat into the chamber. The fire heats the stones so thoroughly and intensely

Permanent stone or adobe brick oven adjacent to sweating chamber

that the heat is conducted through them into the room where the sweating takes place. In some cases, water may not be used, but more often than not, water is poured onto the stones of that heated wall. Often, the water has special medicinal herbs mixed in with it.

Early European Sweat Baths

Where else were sweat baths occurring at the time of Columbus? Although they were not limited to the American continents, it was certainly in North America that the sweat bath was most widespread and most intimately connected with the everyday lives of the native peoples. According to such writers as Ivan Lopatin, in Europe "water-vapor baths," produced by pouring water in heated stones, were primarily confined to the circumpolar regions. The best known of those European water-vapor bath traditions, of course, is the sauna of Finland.

In 425 B.C. Herodotus wrote of the sweat bath customs of the Scythians (whose territory is part of present-day Russia), describing the construction of a sort of sweat lodge: "When they have set up three pieces of wood leaning against each other, they extended around them woolen cloths; and having joined them together as closely as possible, they throw red-hot stones into a vessel in the middle of the pieces of wood and the cloths." Herodotus also described how the Scythians placed certain "fruits" on the fire to inhale the fumes, a custom reminiscent of the Native American practice of placing cedar and sweetgrass on the stones. These baths, Herodotus said, "give off such a vapor as no Grecian vapor-bath can exceed."

According to Homer and other writers among the ancient Greeks (who were passionately fond of bathing), hot air baths called *laconia* (to which Herodotus was referring in the previous quote) were introduced quite early on and the ancient Greek baths all include small laconia. Among the Romans, who loved to copy and exceed the Greeks, these became the Roman *balneum*, small bath chambers using heated water and steam for bathing. In 25 B.C. the Emperor Agrippa built the first giant baths or *thermae*. After the fall of the Roman empire, the idea of steam baths was embraced by the prophet Muhammed around 600 A.D. These Arab *hammams* (from an Arabic word meaning "spreader of warmth") were the parents of the Turkish baths, still found in

Istanbul and in some American cities.

In northern Russia, steam bath houses constructed of wood, sometimes underground or partially submerged in the ground, have been observed and described by travelers from the early centuries of the Christian era to the present day. Lopatin observed that like the Native American sweat lodge, "The Russian water vapor bath serves purposes other than that of mere cleanliness of the body. Even at the present time [1960] peasants use the steam bath for ritualistic purposes, esoteric rites, therapeutic treatment, and even for social affairs." The Russian word for "to take a bath" is *paritsia*, literally "to steam oneself." Among the Russians and the northern Slavs in general, the steam bath predates the introduction of Christianity. The saunas of Finland, Scandinavia, Latvia and Estonia are very much the same as the Russian steam bath. Like the Native American sweat lodge, the Russian sweat bath was not merely recreational but served important social, ceremonial, hygienic and medicinal roles.

Sweat bathing was a Celtic practice as well. Apparently the custom of using a sweat house made of sod and stone began in Ireland somewhere around the eighth century. In an essay entitled "Ancient Irish Hot-Air Bath" published in 1889, Seaton F. Milligan observed that "until recent times the hot-air bath was known over many parts of Ireland as a cure for rheumatism." And in 1892 another paper entitled "An Ancient Irish Hot-Air Bath" was published by Reverend D. B. Mulcahy who found a sweat bath in use on the farm of one Widom M'Curdy. He was told that young women used the sweat bath "to improve their complexion after making peat or pulling flax. . . ."

The similarities between the Russian sweat bath, the sauna (in its original form) and the American Indian sweat lodge are quite striking. They include the use of a very small structure; the lack of ventilation during the sweat experience; the use of switches to strike oneself; the generation of steam by pouring water on heated stones, the use of fragrant herbs; and the mixture of social, therapeutic and ritualistic purposes. As Lopatin puts it:

"Comparing the Sauna type with the American Indian sweat lodge we find them quite similar. They both belong to the same general type and seem to have had an identical origin. Indeed, every characteristic of the Sauna is at the same time a characteristic of the native American steam bath."

Sweat baths have been common in the past in Japan. An interesting description of a Japanese form of sweat bath called the *mushi-buro* (meaning "steam bath") can be found in Aaland's *Sweat*. He also described the *kara-buro* ("empty bath") in which steam is conducted into a chamber and the *todan-buro* ("shelf bath"). Apparently, it is only in Kyoto that these ancient forms of bathing, similar to the Native American sweat lodge, can still be found.

There are also sweating practices in parts of Africa which parallel those of North America. Aaland mentions the steam hut of Liberia. While I was living in West Africa (from 1966 to 1969), I was told by various traditional healers or fetish priests of certain healing ceremonies which would use steam, sometimes from moistened green leafy branches placed in a fire, or direct heat in a small enclosed area to help heal various physical and spiritual ailments. In Ghana, Togo, Benin, and Nigeria, the use of heat and steam to induce sweat as part of therapeutic treatment was, in my experience, widely practiced.

Early Descriptions of
Native American Sweats

Although sweat baths have been part of American Indian life for countless centuries, apparently the first Europeans to write about the Native American sweat bath were the Spanish missionaries who went to Mexico. In the early sixteenth century Diego Duran, a Dominican friar, described Aztecs making extensive use of the *temazcalli* or sweat house. For the Aztecs, the vapor bath was the favorite remedy for almost every ill. "These bath houses," Duran says, "are heated with fire and are like small low huts. Each one can hold ten persons in a squatting position. The entrance is very low and narrow. People enter one-by-one and on all fours." The friars took note of the fact that there was an Aztec god of the temazcalli and that prayers were chanted during these "dry baths." In his chronicle, *Things of New Spain*, Sahagun wrote that it was in the temazcalli that the sick "restore their bodies, their nerves. Those who are as if faint with sickness are there calmed, strengthened."

The Mayan people, like the Aztecs, also made use of sweat baths. Some of the Mayan temples had elaborate sweat baths made of stone. Yaxchilan is one example. Located near the border of present-day Mexico and Guatemala, and built sometime before 900 A.D., it contains eight sweat baths. Each has its own stone-built hearth lined with potsherds, benches made of masonry for those taking the sweat bath and drains built in to carry off water.

It should be noted that those Spaniards (like the French and Dutch and English who would follow them into the New World) were not merely surprised but appalled at the premium the native peoples universally placed on bathing of any kind—whether in water or in steam. In fifteenth-, sixteenth-, seventeenth-, and eighteenth-century Europe, bathing was regarded as unhygienic, even an abomination. According to Siegfried Giedion in his book *Mechanization Takes Control* (Oxford University Press, 1948), for both Catholics and Protestants in Western Europe before 1850, "bath and sin were one. There is no doubt that the most elementary sense of cleanliness was lacking." The eighteenth-century German poet Goethe was ashamed of his own passion for swimming, and at least one of Goethe's friends broke off his relationship with the poet because of Goethe's "foolish superstitions" about bathing and swimming.

This explains, in part, why the Spanish tried so hard to wipe out the customs of sweat lodge and sweat house in their various colonies in North America from Mexico to California, usually with disastrous results for the health of the native peoples. One of the queens of Aragon in Spain boasted that, exempt by birth and marriage, she had never bathed. The aversion to bathing also accounts for the strong interest Europeans of those centuries had in perfumes. The oral traditions of the native peoples of the Americas and Africa mention that one could smell a European coming from some distance away.

The Spanish custom of banning the sweat bath was aided in some cases by the introduction of European diseases which decimated native populations throughout the Americas. As much as 90 percent of the population of Mexico was wiped out by European epidemics between 1500 and 1550. Although sweat baths were effective therapy for many indigenous ailments, fatalities from such diseases as smallpox and measles increase when a sweat is induced. Despite this, the use of sweats endured and, when native people had time to adapt to the new diseases and recognized which ones could not be countered by a sweat bath, the use of the sweat bath may even have increased. Maud Oakes' 1973 study of a highlands Mayan village in Guatemala, *The Two Crosses of Todos Santos*, points out that in the present-day village of Todos Santos every family has its own sweat bath, "a stone and adobe hut large enough for two" and that each person in the village takes at least one sweat bath every week.

The banning of the sweat bath for Native Americans in the sixteenth century and the years that followed might be compared

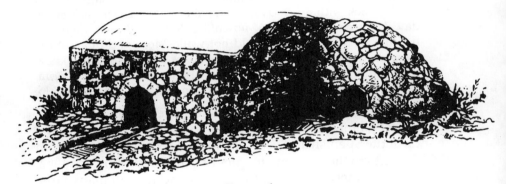

Temescal

to banning *both* communion and the use of antibiotics for contemporary devout Catholics. Oakes' book contains an interview done with an elderly "prayermaker" named Tata Julian who was sent with other Mayan young men to Guatemala City for education. He attributed his rheumatism to the fact that he was unable to take sweat baths while in school:

> In the college we had to bathe in cold water. I went to the chief and said, "Señor, it is the custom in my pueblo for the *naturales* to take sweat baths. Here there is no sweat bath. Will you give me permission to heat a little water for a bath?" He would not give me permission. After I had been there a year and six months, we all became sick with much dysentery. All of us were sick, sick every day. They gave us just tea; no coffee. Many *naturales* died. We became so weak that we could not walk. More and more of the *naturales* died. Then my thoughts went back to Todos Santos. I knew that if I did not escape I would never see my pueblo again. Señorita, as weak as I was I escaped one night and I returned to my pueblo.

To this day, the temescal is still widely used by the contemporary descendants of the Aztecs and Mayans who suffered at the hands of the Spanish and yet still endured. While traveling from Mexico City to the highland jungles of Chiapas Province in 1992, I observed temescals behind the houses and huts in many large and small villages. As innocuous as baking ovens, these temescals are used just as they were in the fifteenth century, even though some of the religious tradition which used to accompany their use may have been lost. In *Tepoztitlan, Village in Mexico,* Oscar Lewis wrote in 1960 of the practice of carrying a woman to the temescal for a sweat bath eight days after she gives birth. "The new baby is also exposed briefly to the steam of the temescal. Almost every woman takes two steam baths; some take the traditional four."

In the early 1600s, a Dutchman named David deVries in the New Netherlands colony (which would later be New York) wrote an account of a Mahican sweat bath (collected in Jameson's *Narratives of New Netherland*):

When they wish to cleanse themselves of their foulness, they go in the autumn, when it begins to grow cold, to make, away off, near a running brook, a small oven, large enough for three or four men to lie in it. In making it they first take twigs of trees, and then cover them tight with clay, so that smoke cannot escape. This being done, they take a parcel of stones, which they heat in a fire, and then put in the oven, and when they think it is sufficiently hot, take the stones out again and go and lie in it, men and women, boys and girls, and come out perspiring, that every hair has a drop of sweat on it. In this state they plunge into the cold water; saying that it is healthy, but I let its healthfulness pass; they then become entirely clean, and are more attractive than before.

Just as in Mexico, sweat lodges were not just for the purpose of personal hygiene. The curative qualities of the sweat lodge were widely known and have long been documented. Healing sweats might be undertaken by an individual (in as matter-of-fact a fashion as we now take an aspirin) or in groups (with considerable ceremony accompanying the sweat).

For one of the earliest European accounts of a healing sweat, we can turn to the Lenape. The Lenape people originally lived in that part of the northeast now known as northern Pennsylvania, New Jersey, and the lower Hudson Valley—including the area of present-day New York City. *Bagnio* was their name for the sweat lodge. William Penn, the founder of Pennsylvania, wrote a very clear description of how a Delaware man named Tenoughan made use of his sweat lodge in the dead of winter in 1683 to cure himself of a fever. Penn wrote in his journal:

> I found him ill of a fever, his Head and Limbs much affected with Pain, and at the same time his Wife preparing a Bagnio for him: The Bagnio resembled a large Oven, into which he crept, by a Door on the one side, while she put several red hot Stones in a small Door on the other side thereof, and then fastened the Doors as closely from the Air as she could. Now while he was sweating in this Bagnio, his wife was, with an Ax, cutting her husband a passage into the River in order to the immersing himself, after he should come out of his Bath. In less than half an Hour, he was in so great a

Sweat, that when he came out, he was as wet as if he had come out of a River, and the Reak or Steam of his body so thick, that it was hard to discern any bodies Face that stood near him. In this condition, stark naked (his Breech-Clout only excepted) he ran to the river, which was about twenty Paces, and duck'd himself twice or thrice therein, and so return'd (passing only through his Bagnio to mitigate the immediate stroak of the Cold) to his own house, perhaps twenty paces further, and wrapping himself in his woolen mantle, lay down as his length near a long (but gentle) Fire in the midst of his wigwam, or House, turning himself several times, till he was dry, and then he rose, and fell to getting us our Dinner, seeming to be as easie, and well in Health, as at any other time.

We find a considerable amount of even earlier information regarding sweat lodges in the *Jesuit Relations,* the yearly reports sent by Jesuit missionaries in "New France"(the present-day Canadian province of Quebec) to their superior in France. While he was doing research in 1993 in the *Jesuit Relations* for the Abenaki Nation of Vermont, my son Jesse Bowman Bruchac discovered a number of interesting descriptions of sweat lodges in "New France." In one of them, LeJeune's *Relation* (1637), the priest observed:

Here is something quite remarkable: towards evening of the 26th, they prepared a sweat, which was followed by a feast. I never saw anything like it in my life; 20 men entered, and almost piled themselves upon one another. Even the sick man dragged himself thither, though with considerable difficulty, and was one of the troop; he also sang for quite a long time, and in the midst of the heat of this sweat he asked for water with which to refresh himself, —a part of which he drank and the rest he threw over his body. An excellent remedy, forsooth, for a sick man on the verge of death! So the next day I found him in a fine condition. . . .

The story which I have retold in this volume as "The Bow Wrapped in Bark" can be found in the *Relation* of Jean de Brebuef for the year 1636. In the *Relation* of Hierosme Lalemant for 1646, a description is given of a medicine man's use of the sweat house to divine the future:

On another occasion, before setting out for war, a medicine man was consulted. A bark sweat house 3 or 4 feet high and wide was built for him and inside were placed hot stones. The medicine man shut himself inside the sweat house and sang while the warriors danced outside. Finally, his spirit gave him the answer and he yelled out, "Victory! I see the enemies coming toward us from the south. I see them take to flight. I see all of you making prisoners of them." On the basis of this, the warriors departed toward the south.

Not all of the Jesuits were so objective in their descriptions of the sweat lodges, however. Another of the accounts which Jesse discovered is from Bressant's *Relation* (1653):

> They use hot baths but in a very Barbarous manner; they inclose large stones, red-hot, in a little cabin, where 15 or 20 persons come together, seated like Apes, who touch one another closely, and remain there during whole hours, —working themselves, while singing violently, into an excessive perspiration; and on issuing thence, even at the beginning of winter, they plunge into some half-frozen lake or river, from which, inexplicable though it seems, they return without distress. They do this from superstition, for cleanliness, for health, and for pleasure; it is thus that they refresh and invigorate themselves in the midst of long journeys, and obviate fatigue upon returning.

This use of a sweat lodge for divination was, apparently, common in the northeast and is much like the "shaking-tent" of both North America and Siberia. Here a shaman does a divination by entering a small tent or lodge where he is bound hand and foot and left inside. The tent soon begins to shake and the shaman's voice and other voices are heard from within. When it is over, the shaman may emerge untied, may still remain bound or may have disappeared from the tent to be found elsewhere in the vicinity.

By the eighteenth century, the sweat lodge was well known to the European colonists of North America. Descriptions of sweat lodges abound in the early accounts. John Smith describes sweat baths among the Virginia Indians. Bossu, in *Travels in the*

Interior, also described it among the Choctaws of Louisiana. They enter "steam cabinets in which are boiled all sorts of medicinal and sweet smelling herbs" and where "the vapors filled with the essence and salts of these herbs enter the patient's body through his pores and his nose and restore his strength." He urged Europeans to follow the Indian custom of doing at least three sweats a year.

Many of those European immigrants did adopt the custom of taking part in native sweats or even having lodges of their own. Sagard in his *Long Journey to the Country of the Hurons* speaks of his countrymen's participation in sweats with some distaste: "I have seen some of our Frenchmen in these sweat-baths along with the savages, and I was astonished that they wished and were able to endure it, and that a sense of propriety did not lead them to hold aloof from it."

In some cases, the idea of the sweat was adopted without most of American culture recognizing that its roots were Native. Virgil J. Vogel in *American Indian Medicine* traces certain techniques involving steam therapy which became common in American medicine directly to Native roots. The vaporizers which are widely used by the bedside of children suffering from the croup are nothing more than a portable approximation of the steam of a sweat bath.

The Repression of the Sweat Lodge

If there are so many connections between the sweat lodge and such European practices as the sauna and the Russian sweat bath, and if at least some Europeans adopted the practice of taking part in Native American sweats as early as the 1600s, we find ourselves faced with two big questions. Why is there still so little knowledge about the sweat lodge in American culture? And why, if many Europeans have a similar tradition and there is some history of Europeans actually using American Indian sweat baths, do many Native Americans object to the use of the sweat lodge by contemporary non-Indians?

I believe that both of those answers may be found in history. First of all, there was the western European aversion—for at least the first several centuries of contact—towards *any* kind of bathing. In this area as in many others, Western European culture and Native American culture were in direct conflict. Sweat bathing was often described as an ignorant, an unhealthy and a savage custom. Secondly, the association of the sweat bath with ceremony contributed to the sweat bath being labeled as yet another instrument of the devil. Native Americans were extremely tolerant of other people's religions and made no attempt to prevent Europeans from practicing their various Christian faiths. Respect for others and non-interference with their ways are important tenets of Native life. The exact opposite was true of the Europeans, who tried every means from slavery to slaughter to extirpate Native American religions. Control, not tolerance, characterizes the European approach to relations with Native Americans.

In California, the Spanish missions controlled virtually every aspect of Native life leading to a drastic decline in the Native population. In the early 1800s, sweat baths were forbidden by the missions. One Spaniard's observation in 1811 of the results of this ban can be found in Arthur Kroeber's 1908 "A Mission Record of the California Indians," which reads:

There is a custom among the men of entering daily a subterranean oven which is called temescal. Into this they bring fire. When it is sufficiently heated, they go in undressed. Then they sweat profusely, so that when they come out they look as if they had been bathing. It is known that this is very beneficial to them. For some time these were forbidden and many itches, tumors, and other epidemics were found among the men. On the sweat houses being given back to them, hardly a man with the itch could be found.

In order to survive, many Native religious practices had to go underground. Because of that historical need to withdraw and protect, it is not easy to be as open to outsiders as it was prior to the last five centuries of genocide. Much of the contemporary secrecy surrounding certain Native ceremonial practices came into being within the last two hundred years. In fact, in the last half of *this* century, many Native American communities have enacted laws forbidding non-Indians to remain in their communities overnight because of continuing bad experiences with whites who still try to control and interfere. As Native self-assurance and religious freedom increase and as non-Natives demonstrate their desire to live *with* Native peoples, not on top of them, the old openness may reassert itself.

Not everyone is familiar with the history of government repression of Native religious practices. The First Amendment states clearly that Congress shall make no laws respecting the establishment of religion or prohibiting the free exercise thereof. Some people find it unbelievable that the United States, founded on the ideals of basic civil rights, continued to deny—by law— many of those rights to the original natives for most of this very century. But the documentation is to be found in the National Archives in Washington, D.C. of case after case in which Native Americans were denied the freedom to publicly congregate, the freedom of speech, and the freedom of worship. Circular No. 1655, dated April 26, 1921, deals with Indian dancing and contains this statement:

Sacred house and sweat house in Karok town of Katimin, Northern California

The sun-dance and all similar dances and so-called religious ceremonies are considered "Indian Offenses" under existing regulations and corrective penalties are provided.

Half a century earlier, in 1873, sweat baths were forbidden to all Native Americans by the Federal government. The ban on most Native ceremonial practices including the sweat lodge continued into the 1930s. These laws were very actively enforced, and there are many cases of Native people being fined or jailed simply because they took part in a sweat lodge. It seems ironic and even obscene to many Native Americans that certain Indians and non-Indians presently are making money by selling the sweat lodge experience when their parents and grandparents were forbidden by law to engage in sweats as a free healing religious sacrament.

Sadly, the attack on Native American religions continues to this day. I strongly recommend an essay by Vine Deloria, Jr. entitled "Trouble in High Places: Erosion of American Indian Rights to Religious Freedom in the United States," which deals with Supreme Court decisions in 1988 and 1990 which impact heavily on Native religious freedom. It can be found in the 1992 anthology *The State of Native America*, edited by M. Annette Jaimes and published by South End Press.

The Seneca leader Sagoyewatha, better known to white America by the name Red Jacket, spoke these words to a Boston missionary two centuries ago, and they are no less true today:

> Brother, our seats were once large, and yours were very small; you have now become a great people, and we have scarcely left a place to spread our blankets; you have got our country, but are not satisfied; you want to force your religion upon us. . . .

> Brother! We do not wish to destroy your religion, or take it from you. We only want to enjoy our own.

THE PARTS OF THE LODGE

The Poles

When the twelve white willow saplings which form the framework of the Lakota inipi are cut, tobacco is placed to show thanks for their sacrifice. Without this acknowledgment of the contribution made by the willows in providing the poles for the lodge, sickness or ill health might come to the person building the lodge and those making use of it. Reverence is usually viewed as an essential part of the preparation of any lodge, whether it be a Lakota inipi or a Havasupai to'olva.

Every part of the preparation of the sweat lodge has special meaning. For example, among the Lakotas, when the poles of the lodge are bent and tied together at the top, the crossing poles form a square with four sides. Those four sides stand for the four directions.

When the framework is completed, the poles make an overarching shape like an overturned basket or a beehive. Now those willow poles are seen symbolically in a number of ways. They are the arch of the sky. They are also the ribs of the sweat lodge being, which is seen in some Native cultures as a turtle, in some as a bear, and among many of the Native nations of the Pacific northwest as the body of the Creator of all things.

Although other saplings were sometimes used, most frequently the poles of a sweat lodge are willow. Melvin Gilmore, the ethnobotanist author of *Prairie Smoke*, a book about the life of the Indians of the Missouri valley, explained the choice of the willows in terms he had learned from the various Native elders who shared their knowledge with him. The willow is a tree which is always found growing along flowing water. It seemed, therefore, that the willow had a special relationship with the water, "the element so immediately and constantly needful to man and to other living things." Water is not only used to "vivify and reanimate," it is also essential for cleansing. Since the willow is a tree connected to moving water, it is highly appropriate that it should be a part of the structure in which water in the form of

Bringing the sweat lodge willows

steam is used for a cleansing that is more than skin deep.

The willow is also a representative of the plant world. The animals, the plants, birds, stones, air, water and fire are all represented in the sweat lodge—which is a microcosm of all creation. Each part of creation has its own special powers and lends those powers to the person in the sweat lodge.

The deciduous trees, such as the willow, have the power of resurrection. They prove their ability to die and be reborn by the process of losing their leaves each year and then waking again with new growth in the spring. Similar symbolic death and rebirth was undergone by the person who went into the sweat lodge, and the presence of the willow surely strengthened that experience.

Willow is also widely known as a medicine tree. Long ago, many different Native American nations learned that willow bark could be used to make a medicine which would cure headaches and other pains. Salicin, the active ingredient in this willow-bark medicine, was synthesized many years later in the Western world to make acetylsalicylic acid—aspirin.

It is also true that willow branches are straight and supple. Willow poles can be bent almost into a complete circle without breaking. So, for many reasons, it is hard to imagine a tree better suited than the willow for the poles of a sweat lodge.

The Covering

There are, as we have already described, many kinds of sweat baths in North America. Although the most familiar form today is the Lakota inipi, sweat baths range from the temescals of Mexico to the cedar sweats of the northwest coast and the bark-covered lodges of the northeastern woodlands. Today, most sweat lodges are not intended as permanent structures, lasting only a few seasons, yet in many parts of North America the lodges were constructed in such a way as to make them at least as sturdy as the dwellings in which the people lived their every-day lives. In the case of the sweat houses of California and some of the sweat baths of the arctic regions, the sweat house was either a permanent part of the house or the house itself. Because of that, the covering of the lodge varied from one place to another.

In the northeast, along the coast, the bottom of the lodge wall might be a stone foundation and above it, the covering would be woven rush mats. In the southeast, a sweat lodge might be dug into the side of a riverbank or a hill near a pond, making the covering of the lodge the earth itself. In Mexico, sweat houses among the Maya are permanent. In the case of the Maya of the village of Todos Santos (according to Maud Oakes' well-known study *The Two Crosses of Todos Santos*), each family would have its own sweat bath in the form of a stone and adobe hut in the yard, which would be used at least twice a week. The ancient Maya built sweat baths into their great buildings of stone. At Yaxchilan, an extensive city from the fifth century A.D. in the very center of the Mayan area of Mexico, there are no fewer than eight sweat baths. These sweat baths had stone built hearths which were lined with potsherds, benches made of masonry for the bathers, and drains used to carry off the water. In California, where the sweat houses of more than fifty different tribal nations did not make use of water on hot stones, the sweat house was often built of wood or wood and earth. When it was not being heated to extreme temperatures, it might serve as a house for the men or as a dwelling place. Sweat houses made of cedar boards and chinked with seaweed were found further north along the Pacific coast.

Today, the most common form of the sweat lodge is that of the Lakota inipi. In the past, among the Plains nations like the Lakota, the inipi would be covered with buffalo hides or the skins of other animals. Today, however, the covering is usually canvas or heavy blankets.

Whatever the lodge's covering was in the past or is today, the symbolism of that covering was more or less universal. When you were within the lodge, the covering was like the night sky above your head. It was also like the skin of a great animal, in whose body you were being held. Or like the skin and body of your own mother in that time when you had not yet been born. A lodge covered with the skin of a powerful animal, like the bear, might have a very special power associated with it. The bear is associated with life and death because of its way of hibernating through the winter. A bear in its sleep is close to the spirit world and a lodge covered with a bear skin is, in some Iroquois stories, a lodge used to bring people back to life.

But once the lodge has been covered, no matter what the covering may be, that lodge becomes a living being. As the story told in the Pacific northwest by many tribal nations—including the Nez Perce, the Yakima, the Okanagan and the Colville—explains, the sweat lodge is the body of the great Spirit Chief who gave the animals their names and transformed into this new shape to help the human beings. Within the lodge, you are within the body of something alive and powerful and in the darkness within that skin of power, you pray for health and life.

Sweat lodge covered with animal skins

The Stones

The stones which are heated in the fire and brought into the lodge are often referred to as our elders. They called by the Lakota *tunka*, and the word *tunka-shila* means "grandfather." The Lakota and other Native people recognize that earth and the stones are alive. The rocks were here before people were here. Lakota traditions say that life began with the rising of a great stone from the waters of creation. When the stones of the sweat lodge are heated and glowing in the dark, we return to that first dawn of creation.

Many traditional tales speak of the age and the wisdom of the stone people. Among the Iroquois of the northeast, the tale of the storytelling stone explains that in the old days stories were not known by human beings. It was not until a great rock began to tell stories to a boy named Gah-gah or "Crow" that storytelling became a part of the human experience. Among the Lakota we have the story of Stone Boy, the child of a woman and a rock, who brings the first inipi to the people. Universally, the stones of the sweat lodge are always treated with respect and spoken to as one would speak to an elder. The Anishinabe say that when the men are gathering the stones for the lodge, they must put down tobacco as an offering. Then they will know which stones are the right ones to use. Those stones are never to be thrown or dropped, and if a heated stone accidentally falls to the ground when being carried from the fire to the lodge, it is usually placed back into the fire and another stone taken in its place.

In addition to a recognition of the sacred nature of the stones used in the lodge, there is a very practical understanding about the kinds of stones to be used for sweats. The best stones for sweats are igneous. Lava rocks hold the heat longest and do not crumble when water is poured on them. This is in contrast to sedimentary rocks or metamorphic rocks which tend to crack into pieces after being used once in a sweat. Round stones are preferred, about the size of a man's head. And stones which have quartz in them, stones which come from river beds, and stones which are white granite, are never to be used in a sweat lodge. Such stones sometimes explode when they are heated and water is poured on them.

The Tanaina and the other Native peoples of Alaska made frequent use of sweat lodges. In the book *Tanaina Tales from Alaska*, Chippewa writer Bill Vaudrin retold a story which has a direct reference to the stones used for the sweat lodge. It is a "tall tale" story of Skaga, a very quarrelsome little chickadee. It begins with Chickadee pestering the river monster (a sort of northern crocodile which Alaskan natives all agree inhabits the river delta region of southern Alaska) until it bites off one of his legs. Chickadee is so thirsty because of this that he goes over to a lake, drinks it all up, goes to another lake and drinks it, too. His stomach is now so big he can't move, so he lies on his back singing and crying for the people to come and get him because he now wants to be one of them. The people take pity on him and come to carry him back up to their village in a caribou skin. But Chickadee refuses. "That skin is too small," he says. Then they bring a bear skin. "That skin is too small," he says again. Finally a wise old woman gets an idea and has them bring down a mouse skin. "Yes," Chickadee says, "that skin is big enough."

So, complaining all the way, Chickadee is carried up to the village. But when they start carry him into their *gazhee*, a circular poled skin-covered house, Chickadee stops them. "That door is too small." They try door after door until the wise old woman finally understands. "Get a needle," she tells them. "That will be big enough. So they get a bone needle and bring Chickadee in to the gazhee through the needle's eye. They put him down by the fire, but Chickadee is not happy. He keeps complaining and complaining that the fire is not hot enough. Finally one of the men in the village loses his temper, picks up a piece of white granite stone, and throws it on the fire. The white stone explodes from the heat and a tiny piece of granite pierces Chickadee's stomach. Immediately all of the water Chickadee drank from those two lakes comes rushing out and drowns everyone in the village except for the wise old woman who escapes by climbing into a clam shell. As funny as the story may seem, it serves as a teaching tale. It makes it very easy for anyone who has ever heard it to remember not to place white granite stones into the fire in order to heat them for a sweat lodge.

The Pipe

Not all Native sweat lodges involve the use of the pipe. But the pipe is used in so many of them, especially in the Lakota inipi (the most common form of sweat lodge today), that it is important to speak about it. In most Lakota sweats, the pipe is smoked within the lodge each time the door of the lodge is opened and it is kept on the altar outside the lodge when the doorflap is closed.

It is also important to speak about the pipe because a great many non-Native people, including those fascinated by Native culture, have little understanding about the meaning of the pipe and what, among the people who have the pipe tradition, it means to be a pipe carrier. Making and selling things has long been a part of Native life—well before Columbus there were trade routes across North and Central America which brought not only food and household goods from one Native culture to another but also provided items used in sacred and ceremonial ways such as pipestone and parrot feathers. Therefore it is not uncommon today to walk into a store selling "Indian arts and crafts" and find a pipe for sale. Native people also can be found selling pipes at pow-wows and craft fairs. However, just because someone can buy a pipe does not mean that person knows the right way to use it. One common saying among Native people today is this: "Sacred knowledge is not for sale."

Perhaps a person from Western culture might understand it better in these terms. If you are a Catholic and you take communion, it has meaning because it is done in a sacramental setting by a priest who is ordained. What if, however, "Catholic-ism" became as interesting to popular culture as "Indians" are? What would a devout Catholic think of businesses selling communion wafers and the vestments of priests to non-Christians so that at special "authentic" ceremonies, for a price, they could learn to "give communion" dressed in those robes bought from the "Catholic Arts and Crafts Store"?

Just as you cannot learn any religious tradition solely from a book, these few words about the pipe cannot begin to tell you everything that the pipe means to Native people. But, like Black Elk's words recorded by Joseph Epes Brown in *The Sacred Pipe*, they may lead people towards respect and understanding for Native traditions.

There are many different traditions about the sacred pipe, just as there are many different ways of doing sweats from one Native nation to another. Once again, I want to emphasize the diversity of the original Native cultures of this continent. In most of them, though, as with the Lakota, the pipe and the tobacco are used to help send prayers up to the Creator.

The story of White Buffalo Calf Woman illustrates the importance of the sacred pipe to the Lakota people. (More complete tellings of the coming of White Buffalo Calf Woman and the sacred pipe can be found in a number of books, including Black Elk's *The Sacred Pipe, Lame Deer, Seeker of Visions* by John Fire and Richard Erdoes and *Cante Ohitika Win [Brave-Hearted Women]: Images of Lakota Women from the Pine Ridge Reservation,* edited by Carolyn Reyer and published by University of South Dakota.)

> Long ago, two young men were out hunting. It had been a bad winter and the people were starving. All day they searched for buffalo, but they saw no sign of any animals. Then, at the end of the day, they saw a figure coming toward them. It was a beautiful woman, dressed all in white buckskin. She carried sage in her hands and carried a bundle on her back. She told them she had been sent by the Buffalo Nation to help them.
>
> One of the young hunters felt lust in his heart as he saw her and he reached out to grab her. As he did this, a white cloud covered him and when it lifted, all that was left of the man was bones. The other young man's thoughts were pure and he was told by the woman to return to his people and have them make ready for her arrival the next day by building a medicine lodge.
>
> He did as she said and on the next day the woman came to their camp, holding in her hands a large pipe and a small round stone. The bowl of the pipe was made of red stone. Long ago, that stone

had been the blood of ancient animals. It stood for the stones, for the Earth, and for those ancient beings. On the pipe was carved the shape of a buffalo to stand for the Buffalo Nation. Twelve eagle feathers hung from the pipe, a symbol of the eagle, which is the messenger of Wakan-Tanka, the Great Spirit. The stem of the pipe was carved of wood and stood for the trees and the plants which give life. Then she showed the people how to smoke the pipe, how to use it to send a voice to Wakan-Tanka with the smoke from the pipe. When they prayed with the pipe, she told them, they would pray for everything and with everything.

Then White Buffalo Calf Woman gave them the small round stone. On it were seven circles, ranging in size from a large circle to a very small one. Those circles represented the seven sacred ceremonies which she then taught them. Those ceremonies are the soul keeping ceremony in memory of the death of a loved one, the sun dance, the vision quest, the sweat lodge, the puberty rite for women, the making of relatives, and the sacred ball game.

When she had finished teaching the people, White Buffalo Calf Woman walked in a circle and left the medicine lodge. She walked away, stopped, sat down and when she stood she was a black buffalo calf. She walked further, sat down and when she arose she was a brown buffalo calf. A third time she walked and sat and rose up as a red buffalo calf. The last time she stopped and sat, she arose as a white buffalo calf and then disappeared over the western horizon.

Stoking the fire chamber for an after-childbirth session

CREATION

First Sweat
for the Sun Dancers

Rain falls
through thin leaves of late summer
cold on our skins

stones from a wall
my great-grandfather piled
have turned white with heat
from the fire of logs
once stacked chest-high

within the sweat lodge
Crow Dog's voice
speaks to the grandfathers
and the hiss of water
whispered against stones
glowing in the center
is the voice of the earth
at the time when Creation
first turned to life

my sons on each side
bent sapling against my back
we go into the darkness together
six stones added to sixteen
cedar needles fall and rise
in smoke, burning eyes into vision

and then we sing, together we sing
words we did not know we knew
heat driving foreheads down
to touch the mats of woven grass
brought from West Africa

44

breath goes shallow as moist heat
burns our backs
the touch of a flaming wing
until the blanket lifts
and we realize we have been seeing
each other with only our ears and our skins
that the prayers we heard each other offer
were not spoken by our lips

and when Sitting Bull's pipe
circles the lodge, glowing like the rising sun
passed to me by my son's hand
passed on to my other son
I realize in many ways what it means to sing
We shall live again
We shall live again

Fire is associated with creation in so many cultures that it should not be surprising to find that not only the sweat lodge which is heated by fire, but also the sweat which comes from the heated skin should be associated with creation. In some of the stories of Native North America, the relationship of the sweat lodge to creation may be somewhat indirect—for example, the sweat lodge being one of the first things created. In the Okanagan story, the Creator transforms himself into the sweat lodge to be able to give help more directly to human beings.

However, in other cases, as in a multitude of stories told by the Native peoples of California, the sweat lodge existed before creation. The Creator, known as "The Giver" in this tale, and a companion are found living in a sweat house in the midst of the mist long before the creation of the waters and the earth. To make human beings, the Giver goes into the sweat house, lies down and sweats. It is from that sweat that the humans are formed.

An interesting parallel to this can be found in Hindu mythology. Shiva, one of the Hindu triumvirate of primary gods, is known as a being associated with human fertility and as a destroyer. One day, Shiva is out walking and begins to sweat. He wipes the sweat from his body with a cloth and then throws the cloth on the ground. From the sweat in that cloth, a woman is born.

Because the sweat lodge is so often described as a womb and because the experience of leaving the lodge is often equated with being reborn, it is clear why sweat lodges seem to be universally linked to stories and ideas of creation. When one is within the lodge, in the presence of the flowing lava stones, and the steam which rises as it must have risen from the molten surface of the earth when the first rain fell long, long ago, one comes to a very personal understanding of the logical and spiritual connections with creation which are offered by the experience of the sweat.

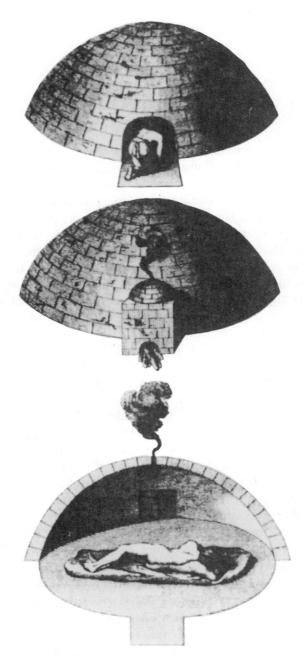

Temescal depicted by Francesco Clavigero, 1787

Noogami's Arrival
(Micmac)

There was Geezoolgh, the Creator, the one who was made, the one responsible for making everything. First Geezoolgh made the sun, Nisgam, our grandfather. The sun was made and it was in the shape of a circle and it moved in a circle. Then Geezoolgh made Oositgamoo, the place where we all are, the earth.

After the sun and the earth were made, a bolt of lightning struck the earth. From that bolt of lightning, Glooskap was formed. He was there, lying on the earth, his head toward the rising sun, his feet toward the setting sun. The lightning flashed again, striking a dry tree, and now there was light and Glooskap could see. He saw the plants and the animals and everything around him, but he could not move.

"When can I get up?" Glooskap said.

"I will tell you when to rise," Geezoolgh said.

Then lightning struck a third time and Glooskap stood up in the form of a human. He went to the east and then to the west. He went to the north and then to the south. He looked up and gave thanks to Geezoolgh, the Creator and Nisgam, the sun. He looked down and gave thanks to Oositgamoo, the earth.

Glooskap began to wander around then. He wandered all over the earth. He saw all the animals and birds and the plants and he saw that everything was beautiful, but he wondered about what he was supposed to do. "What shall I do?" Glooskap asked the Creator.

"You will meet someone," the Creator said. "You will not be alone then and you will know what to do."

Glooskap continued to wander until he saw someone. It was an old woman. "I am Noogami, your grandmother," she said.

"Where have you come from, Grandmother?" Glooskap said.

The old woman smiled. "I came from the stones, grandson. In the morning I was a rock on the ground, but when the sun was at his strongest, in the middle of the day, his heat gave me strength

48

and the shape of an old woman. Now I have come to bring you wisdom. Listen to me and you will know what to do. Because I am so old, I know what things are good things to do."

So Glooskap's grandmother, Noogami, arrived to give him wisdom. And whenever Glooskap needed to know what to do, he always learned what was good from his grandmother.

So, when the fire is lit for the sweat lodge, it represents the power of Geezoolgh, the Creator and the power of Nisgam, the sun, and the power of the lightning which struck the earth and created Glooskap. The stones which are heated in that fire remind us of the stone which was given life by the heat of the sun and became Noogami.

Within the circle of the sweat lodge, a circle like the shape of the sun and the path the sun follows, the heat of those stones will help us know what is good. They will teach us the wisdom of Noogami, our first and wisest grandmother.

The Creation of the Sweat Lodge
(Dineh [Navajo])

Locust was the first one to enter the Fourth World. There had been three worlds before this one, but each one was destroyed because of wrongdoing. There was water everywhere and monsters everywhere when Locust came up from a hole in the earth.

"Where are you from?" one of the monsters asked.

"I am from the world below this Glittering World," Locust said. "There are other beings behind me who wish to emerge into this world, too."

"No one can live here unless you pass two tests," the monster said. "First, you must stay in one place without moving for four days."

"That is easy," said Locust. Then, as locusts have always done, he shed his skin and left it standing there so that it appeared he was not moving. While the monster watched Locust's skin, Locust went back down through the hole in the earth where all the others were waiting.

"This next world is a beautiful one," Locust said. "Soon you will all be able to join me there." Locust rested until the four days had almost passed and then went back up. While the monster was not looking, Locust dropped his shed skin down the hole and took its place.

"I have passed this test," Locust said. "What is the next one?"

"This test is one you will not pass," the monster said. It took an arrow, swallowed it, and pulled it out the other end of its body. "Can you do this?"

"I will do it the hard way," said Locust. "I will pass it through my body from side to side." Then Locust took the arrow and slid it under his wing covers so that it seemed to pierce his body and come out the other side. "Can you do this?" he said.

The monster knew it was defeated. "You have passed the test. The other beings can enter this world."

Now First Man and First Woman emerged. They shaped dry

land and the four sacred mountains from soil they had gathered in the Third World. They decorated the mountains to make them beautiful. On Sis Naajini, the mountain of the east, they placed white shell and told Dawn Boy to enter there. Bear was told to guard his doorway. On Tzoodzil, the mountain of the south, they placed turquoise and told Turquoise Girl to live there. Big Snake was told to guard her doorway. On Dook'o'oosliid, the mountain of the west, they placed an abalone shell blanket and told Abalone Shell Boy to live there. Black Wind was told to guard his doorway. On Dibe Nitsaa, the mountain of the north, they placed an obsidian blanket and told Obsidian Girl to live there. Lightning was told to guard her doorway.

Then the Holy People decided that they needed to have fire. They talked about how fire was to be made. One of them had brought flint from the Third World and they used that flint to strike a spark and make fire. They gathered wood from four directions and from four trees. With that wood—fir, spruce, juniper and pinion—they fed the first fire in the Fourth World.

Now that they had fire, the men decided that they must make a Tacheeh, a sweat bath. They made it in the shape of a hogan and all the men crowded inside. But even though they heated stones and brought them into the sweat bath, it would not get hot. Then Lightning spoke.

"This sweat bath will not get hot because the doorway is open. We must close it with blankets," Lightning said.

People went to get blankets. With those blankets, they closed the door of the sweat house and it grew hot inside. As the heat increased, First Man began to chant and sing and pray. His songs and prayers and chants became those to be used in the Tacheeh. The Dineh people use those ceremonial chants and prayers in the sweat bath to this day.

The Giver
(Joshua)

There was no land in the beginning. There was only sky and fog and water and the water was still. By that water, a sweat house stood and in that sweat house there lived two men—the Giver and his friend. The friend of the Giver had tobacco. While the Giver remained in the sweat house, his friend stayed outside watching.

As he watched, it seemed as if something was coming.

"Something strange is coming," he said to the Giver. "It looks to be land. Two trees are growing on it."

The Giver's friend continued to watch. He could see that white land was approaching them. The ocean began to move and the land was brought closer. The western part of the land struck the sweat house and stopped. Then it began to stretch to the north and to the south. That land was white as snow and there was no grass upon it. To the south a redwood tree grew. To the north an ash tree grew. The fog began to melt away and now the Giver's friend could see far in every direction. It seemed to him that things were ready now and he went into the sweat house.

"Giver," he said, "are you ready?"

"Is the land solid?"

"It is not quite solid yet."

The Giver took some tobacco and began to smoke. He blew tobacco smoke on the land and the land stopped moving. Five times, the Giver smoked. He smoked while he and his friend talked about how they might create the world and the people. Then night came for the first time and after that daylight appeared. For four days, the Giver worked. The trees began to bud. Grass came up and leaves appeared on the trees. Then the Giver walked around that piece of land which had stopped near his sweat house and as he walked he told the ocean to withdraw and be calm. That is how things began.

Chilula sweat house

The Naming of the Animals
(Okanagan)

Long ago, Great Chief called the animals together.

"New people are coming to this world," Great Chief said, "you all must have names. When the first light shows tomorrow, come to my lodge and you can choose any name you want as long as you are the first one to ask for it."

Coyote listened to what Great Chief said. He already had a name, but it was not a name that he liked. Everyone called him Sin-ka-lip, which means "The Imitator." As soon as Great Chief finished speaking, Coyote knew that he wanted to be the first to come to Great Chief's lodge with the first light to get a new name, a powerful name.

Coyote began to walk around, bragging about the new name he would choose. "Tomorrow, when I am the first to come to Great Chief's lodge, I will pick the most powerful name of all. Maybe I will pick Grizzly Bear. Maybe I will pick Eagle. But everyone will hear my name and know that I am the one in charge of everything."

"Sin-ka-lip," said Coyote's wife, "why do you want to change your name? Are you not happy with being who you are?"

"Tomorrow," Coyote said, ignoring his wife's words, "I will have the most powerful name of all the animals."

Coyote bragged so much that his wife became worried. "If Sin-ka-lip gets a new powerful name," she thought, "he will not be happy living with me and he will leave me."

Coyote bragged and bragged until it was late at night. Then, finally, Coyote decided it was time for him to sleep. "Wake me before the first light of dawn," he said to his wife. "Then I will be sure I get the best name."

But Coyote's wife, afraid that Coyote would not stay with her if he became too powerful, did not do as he asked. Instead, when the dawn came, she let him sleep. In fact, he slept all through the day until it was twilight. Then, finally, she woke her husband.

"This is good," Coyote said, "the sun is not even up yet. I will surely be the first to get to Great Chief's lodge." He ran as fast as he could and he was pleased when he reached the lodge and saw no other animals were there. "Those lazy ones are all still asleep," Coyote laughed. "It is clear that I was meant to be in charge."

Then Coyote walked into Great Chief's lodge. To the side of Great Chief was a stick. On that stick Great Chief had placed many rings, each one with a name on it and the most powerful names near the top. Now, however, only one ring remained.

"Great Chief," Coyote said. "I will be Eagle."

"That name is gone," Great Chief said.

"I knew that," said Coyote, even though he was surprised. "I meant that I will be Grizzly Bear."

"That name, too, has been taken," said Great Chief.

Coyote was very surprised, but he recovered quickly. "Then I will be Salmon," Coyote said.

"That name is gone," said Great Chief. "All of the names but one have been taken." He lifted the stick with the one ring on it. "It is the name at the very bottom. No one else wanted it. It is Sin-ka-lip. It is your name."

Coyote sat down by the fire, unable to say anything. But Great Chief was not yet done.

"Sin-ka-lip," Great Chief said, "everyone has their own job to do. The one who comes last is the one who must take care of everything that is left to do. So your name is a very powerful name. The new ones who are coming are the human beings. There are many monsters who wish to kill them. It will be your job to rid the earth of those monsters. When you do not know what to do, you must look inside yourself for help."

Great Chief meant that Coyote should look into his heart, but Coyote was so excited that he did not listen closely and he thought that Great Chief was telling him to look inside his stomach. So, to this day, Coyote often looks to his stomach for guidance.

"Your job will not be easy," Great Chief said, "and things will not be easy for the human beings who are coming soon to the earth. So I give you a special medicine power. Because you will be fighting many monsters—and because you also seem to make many mistakes—there will be times when you will be killed. But if even one hair is left from your body, your brother Fox can bring you back to life by stepping over what is left of you five times."

Coyote was so happy that he was ready to rush out right away and do something foolish so that he would find out what it was like to die and be brought back to life. But Great Chief was not yet finished.

"The human beings are going to need much help. So I am going to change myself into something which will help them. There is one name left which was not on this pole and so I must take that name. That name is Quil-sten, The One Who Warms. I will not longer have eyes or arms and legs, for I will be Sweat Lodge. When the humans need guidance, they can use me. Whoever wants to build me can seek my help. My ribs will arch over the people and I will hear whatever they say. I will help the people when they are troubled and when they are sick. That will always be my job."

And so, when he finished speaking, Great Chief became Sweat Lodge. That is how the animals got their names, Coyote got his medicine power, and Quil-sten, the sweat lodge, came to be. That is how it happened way back then. That is how it is to this day.

Earth Namer
(Maidu)

Water was everywhere in the beginning. Then Turtle came floating out of the north on a raft. A rope made of feathers fell from the
sky and down that rope came Earth Namer. He climbed into the
raft with Turtle and for a long time, neither of them spoke.

Finally Turtle said, "Where did you come from?"

"I came from the sky," Earth Namer said.

"I would like to get out of the water," Turtle said. "Can you
make land?"

Earth Namer said nothing and again, for a long time, they sat
there.

"When will there be people?" Turtle finally said.

"I need earth to make dry land," said Earth Namer. "Who will
get me some earth?"

"Tie your rope to me and I will dive down under the water.
There is earth down there. When I jerk the rope twice, pull me
back to the surface."

Earth Namer wrapped the rope around Turtle and he dove
down into the water until he was out of sight. Then Earth Namer
waited. Days passed and still he waited. Finally, after years had
passed, the rope in Earth Namer's hands jerked twice. He pulled
for a long time and at last Turtle came up. He was covered with
green slime.

"Where is the earth you brought up?" said Earth Namer.

"It is under my fingernails," said Turtle.

Earth Namer took out his stone knife and scraped the earth
from under Turtle's fingernails. He rolled it into a ball and placed
it on the raft. He looked at it once and it was twice as big. He
looked at it a second time and it was larger than the raft itself. He
looked at it a third time and it was even larger. He looked at it a
fourth time and it was as large as the world is today.

Then Earth Namer and Turtle stepped onto the earth.

"Look east," Earth Namer said. "My sister, Sun, is rising."

Then Sun came up from the east and there was light everywhere.

The day passed and, as darkness began to fall, Earth Namer spoke again. "Look," he said, "my brother Moon is rising." Then Moon came and there was light in the night sky.

Earth Namer called the names of the stars and placed them in the sky. Earth Namer made the great oak tree with many acorns. He traveled all over the world in the shape of a ball of fire making things. Coyote came out of the ground with Rattlesnake, who was Coyote's dog. Plants and birds and animals were made, and all were allowed to make their own houses.

Earth Namer's house was the first sweat house. There was no fire burning in it, but it was as hot as a sweat house should be.

As Earth Namer and Coyote sat in that sweat house Earth Namer said, "Now I will make human beings." He mixed red dirt with water and shaped a man and then a woman from that red dirt. He placed the man on his right side and the woman to his left side on the floor of the sweat house.

"Now I will sweat," said Earth Namer. He lay down on his back and sweated while Coyote sat and watched. The woman and the man began to move, but Earth Namer did not move. He continued to sweat throughout the night. Finally, just before dawn, he sat up. He took a greasewood stick and thrust it into the earth at the center of the sweat house. That stick began to burn and it filled the sweat house with light. Coyote and Earth Namer looked at first man and first woman and first man and first woman looked back at them.

The first man was Kuksu. The first woman was Morning Star Woman. Earth Namer made them in the sweat house.

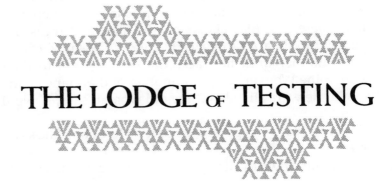

THE LODGE of TESTING

The Lodge of Testing

The sweat lodge is a place of testing. Anyone who has ever been in a sweat understands that aspect of the lodge—those moments when you feel that you cannot stand it any longer and that you have to get out. If you are not calm within a sweat lodge your fears intensify your discomfort, whether that discomfort is real or imagined. Conquering those fears and completing a sweat makes the experience a more meaningful one. You have truly faced your greatest enemy—yourself.

So, it is in the sweat lodge that protagonists in many of the traditional tales of Native North America are tested. It is by passing the test of the sweat lodge that the hero twins of the Dineh prove their worthiness to the Sun Father. The northwestern story of the men who forget the dipper for the lodge shows three friends testing each other's power. In the tales of the northeastern woodlands it is frequently in the sweat lodge that enemies are vanquished.

There is, for example, a Micmac story which was first written down by Silas Rand in 1894 and then retold by Ruth Holmes Whitehead in 1988 in her book *Stories From The Six Worlds*. In that story, a person named Plawej, or "Spruce Grouse," pursues shape-changers who have murdered his wife and his best friend. He follows their trail until he comes to a cliff where he sees a knee sticking out of the stone. One of the shape-changers is trying to hide there. But Plawej cuts off the knee and traps the shape-changer in the rock forever. He defeats the shape-changers one after another until he tracks the last of them to the cave of Porcupine Woman, the grandmother of the shape-changers.

"If he were still alive," the old woman says, "I would roast him."

Then Plawej steps into the cave. "Here I am," he says. "Roast me."

He sits down by the fire and Porcupine Woman glares at him.

Then she calls up the fire and piles hemlock bark and cedar bark on the fire to make it grow hot. The cave is now a sweat lodge and she makes it hotter and hotter until the cave walls start to melt. But Plawej just smiles at her until she has burned up the last of the bark.

"Now it is my turn," he says.

He gathers fuel and builds up the fire. He closes up the mouth of the cave and uses his power to make the fire grow even hotter. The shape-changers beg for mercy from inside the cave, but Plawej pays no attention as his enemies perish.

Like the tale of Plawej, the following stories all illustrate the testing nature of the sweat lodge.

The Bow Wrapped in Bark
(Huron)

Long ago, a young man became ill. He became so ill that it seemed he would die. This young man was the nephew of the Garihoua Andionxra, the great chief of the Bear Nation, so this young man, whose name was Sondaqua, had high standing among his people. He was also known to be brave and steadfast in his actions and so the Arendiwane, the medicine man, came quickly to the lodge of Sondaqua's family to find out what had made the young man sick.

"What have you dreamed?" the Arendiwane asked Sondaqua, who lay sweating in his bed. As soon as he asked this question, the young man seemed to grow stronger.

"I have dreamed that I held a great bow wrapped in bark," Sondaqua said.

"Then you must get that bow," the Arendiwane said. "We will speak of how to do this in the morning."

As soon as the medicine man spoke those words, Sondaqua fell asleep and slept peacefully through the night. When the next day came, the Arendiwane brought the young man to the Council House where the people had assembled.

"I have dreamed that I must get a bow wrapped in bark. There is only one person on earth who has such a bow. I must go to the west to find him. Who will travel with me?"

Many other young men said they would follow Sondaqua and they set out on their journey. They traveled for a long time, always in the direction of the setting sun, the direction of the land of souls. They saw no game at all as they traveled and first one and then another of the young men lost heart and turned back. By the end of ten days, of the many who began the journey, only six remained. Then Sondaqua saw a small black animal on the trail ahead of them.

"We must follow that animal's tracks," Sondaqua said.

They went on for many more days, following the tracks of the

62

small black animal. At last they came to the bark house of the man Sondaqua sought.

"You are welcome," said the man. "I know why you have come and you may have what you desire. But listen well to me. You must keep your minds fixed firmly on what you came here for. And when my wife offers you food, do not eat the first things you are given."

Sondaqua and his five companions followed the man into his bark lodge and he seated them in the place of honor. Then a woman came into the lodge with a bark tray covered with dishes filled with food. The young men had not eaten for many days, but when Sondaqua took his dish and threw it on the ground, the others all did the same. As soon as the dishes struck the earth, it could be seen that they were filled not with food but with poisonous snakes.

Then the woman came back with a second tray of food. This time, Sondaqua and the others took the food and ate it and it was good.

When they had finished their meal, their host took down from the rafters above the fire a great black bow wrapped in bark.

"Whoever hunts with this bow will always be able to bring home game animals. The one who bends this bow tomorrow will own it."

When the next day came, each of Sondaqua's friends one after another, tried, but could not bend the bow. Then Sondaqua took it and the bow bent easily.

The bow is yours," said their host. "Now we must sweat together."

He took the young men outside to the place where his sweat lodge was to be. Stones were piled red hot in the middle of a large fire and their host took the stones out with his bare hands and placed them in a pile. He took saplings, stuck them in the ground in a circle around the hot stones, bent them over waist-high and tied them together at the top. Then he and the young men squeezed into the space between the bent saplings and the hot stones. As soon as they had squeezed in, large pieces of bark and animal skins came from nowhere and covered over the lodge and all was dark except for the glow of the stones.

Their host began to sing then. As he sang, Sondaqua and the five other young men kept their minds firmly on their task. Their job was to bring the bark covered bow back to their people. The lodge grew hotter and hotter and the young men chanted as one is supposed to chant in a lodge.

"Het, het, het!" they chanted loudly.

Throughout the sweat, all of Sondaqua's friends but one kept their minds firmly on their task. That young man thought instead of how hard their journey had been to come to this place. He thought of how easy it would be to just stay here and not return to his people.

When the sweat was over, they all came out of the lodge to go and bathe in the river. The last one to leave the lodge was the young man who had thought of how much easier it would be to stay. As he stood, he raised up his arms and began to grow taller and change in shape. His friends turned to look at him. He was no longer a young man. He was now a tall pine tree.

Then their host showed Sondaqua and his remaining friends the path to travel back to their homes. "Along your way you will pass through woods where there are many game animals. The moose and deer and bear will be as numerous as the leaves on the trees. With your bow you will be able to provide for your village."

And so it was. Sondaqua and his friends returned to their village with the bow rolled in bark and enough game to feed the people for the whole winter.

The Hero Twins
(Dineh [Navajo])

Monster Slayer and Child of Water were the twin sons of Changing Woman. They lived long ago, before the human beings, at a time when there were many monsters in the world. When they were grown, their mother told them that their father was Johanaa'ei, the Sun. So they decided to go and seek his help to destroy the monsters.

Their journey to their father's hogan was a long and hard one. They were helped along the way by Niłch'i, the Wind, who came and whispered advice to them when they were in trouble. At last they reached Johanaa'ei's hogan, but he did not believe the twins were his children. He decided to test them, and one of his tests was to place them in his sweat lodge.

"I will make a sweat bath for you," Sun said. Then he called to his daughter, "Go out and prepare the sweat house," he told her. "Heat for it four of the hardest boulders you can find. Heat a white boulder and a blue boulder, a yellow boulder and a black boulder."

The daughter did as Sun said, but according to some of the versions of this story, she believed that the boys were his children and decided to help them. When she made the sweat house, she dug a small hole at the back of it and covered it with sheet of darkness and white shell so it would be hidden.

"I have made a pit in the back of the sweat house," she whispered to the boys. "You will be safe there."

In another version of the story, it is their friend Niłch'i, the wind who saved them. He watched the sweat house being made and he began to dig a tunnel into the bank toward the back of the sweat house. When he was through, he covered the hole with a flat stone and then whispered to the boys.

"I have made a tunnel for you to hide in," Wind said. "Just move the flat stone and crawl inside. But do not go into the tunnel until after your father has asked his questions and you have answered him."

As soon as the stones were red hot, Sun placed the boys in the sweat house and covered the door with four sky blankets. He put the red dawn blanket over the door, he placed the blue sky blanket over the door, he placed the yellow blanket of evening over the door, and last he placed the black blanket of night over the door. All was dark inside and the boys climbed into the pit in the back of the lodge.

"Are you hot?" Sun said to them from outside the sweat house.

"No," both boys answered, "it is not that hot in here."

Four times he asked and four times they said no. Then Sun climbed up on top of the lodge and began to pour water down onto the hot stones in the middle of the sweat house. The whole lodge filled with scalding hot steam. It was so hot that any human being would be killed, but the twins had crawled into the tunnel at the back of the lodge as soon as they finished answering Sun's questions. So the steam did not harm them.

As soon as the heat had died down, the boys crawled out of the tunnel back into the sweat house.

Sun waited for a while before he spoke again. "Are you hot now?" he said, certain that he would get no reply.

"Yes," both boys answered, "It is hot now, but not as hot as before." Then Sun removed the four blankets from the door and told the boys to come out. When they emerged from the lodge, they stood up tall and strong, unharmed by their ordeal.

Now Johanaa'ei, the sun, began to think the boys were his children.

Me'jo and the Bear
(Naskapi)

One day, Me'jo the Old Man was out walking around. He walked until he came to the big mountain. He began to walk around the mountain and there on the path before him was a great bear. In those days bears were much larger than today. They were terrible monsters who hunted the human beings. If they saw any human being they would surely eat that person. The bear reared up on its hind legs and walked toward Me'jo.

"What are you going to do?" Me'jo said.

"I am going to eat you," said the great bear.

"Wait," said Me'jo. "There is something I must do first. I must take a sweat bath. It is a difficult thing to do, but if you are brave, you can join me. Then, after we are through, you can eat me."

"That is good," said the bear. "I am afraid of nothing. I will join you in this thing."

Then Me'jo made a small cabin from logs. He chinked all the cracks with moss and dirt. He made a door of tightly woven branches. He made a fire and placed stones in the fire. When the fire had burned a long time and the stones were red hot, he peeled the bark from two green forked sticks and used them to move the rocks into the center of the small cabin. Then Me'jo stripped off his clothing, but the bear could not take off its own heavy coat.

"Now we must go in," Me'jo said, "unless you are afraid."

"I am afraid of nothing," said the bear, and he followed Me'jo into the small cabin."

"I will sit here," Me'jo said, taking a seat to the side of the door. "You will sit there, at the back of this lodge." The bear sat down and the lodge was hot.

"Is it too hot?" Me'jo asked.

"It is not too hot," said the bear, but he panted as he spoke.

"That is good," Me'jo said. "Now I will close the door."

"What?" said the bear, panting even harder. "Oh, close the door. Go ahead." Me'jo closed the door and the lodge grew hotter still.

"Is it too hot?" Me'jo asked.

It was hard now for the bear to breathe, but the bear would not admit that Me'jo was stronger. "It is not too hot," the bear said.

Then Me'jo lifted the bucket he had made of birch bark and filled with water.

"If you are not too hot," Me'jo said, "I will pour on water. But it you are afraid, you can leave."

"I am not afraid," the bear panted. "Pour on water. Let it be hot."

Then Me'jo began to sing. He poured water on the stones and they sang with him. Steam rose and filled the lodge and it became very hot indeed.

"Is it too hot now?" Me'jo asked.

But the bear could not answer. He was dead.

So it is that Me'jo brought the first sweat house to the Naskapi and the Montagnai people. And from that time on the Naskapi and the Montagnai people would go into the sweat house and sing to make themselves ready before hunting the great bear.

"Me'jo and the Great Bear" can be read as a guide to proper behavior and the use of the sweat lodge. It is a story which carries in it a number of lessons. It certainly illustrates some of the proper attitudes one must take into a sweat lodge, where humility and self-awareness are more important than bravery or boasting. Me'jo may be a Trickster, but he knows enough to remove his clothes before entering the lodge.

Within the sweat lodge, you are not proving yourself to anyone other than yourself, and what you do is between yourself and the Creator. Because of his lack of self-awareness and his pride, the bear loses his life. From then on, it is the bear who is hunted by the people. But it is also true that before they hunt the bear, the hunters must go into the sweat house and cleanse themselves, since the bear is still a powerful and great animal, one deserving respect. The sweat lodge is both a cleansing ceremony and a responsibility. "Every bear," an old Cree hunter once said, "is a chief."

While traveling in Labrador in the summer of 1920, a man named William Cabot observed that the old Naskapi man who was guiding him, the chief of the St. Augustine band, engaged in the sweat bath more than thirty times during the six weeks they were together. The sweat bath was, in those days, a central part of a hunter's life.

Not only is the human scent, which animals might avoid, cleansed from your body, but you are also made clean in spirit and in mind. I have been told by friends among the James Bay Cree that such sweats to purify themselves before going out to hunt the game animals have remained an important part of the lives of northern hunters.

Koso sweat lodge

The Beaver Stick
(Blackfeet)

Back in the time before horses came to the people there lived a young man. His parents had died when he was very young. An old woman cared for him for a while, but she too died while he was still in his youth. Because his clothes were so tattered, the people of the village called him by the name Manyan as a joke, since Manyan means "new robe."

Because Manyan had no one to care for him or teach him how to care for himself, his hair was always matted and dirty. His bow was an old one, so weak that a man could throw an arrow further than it could shoot one. Moreover his arrows had blunt points and bent shafts, and his only knife was a flint blade so dull that it could cut nothing.

Yet despite his misfortune, Manyan was always happy, He did not think himself to be less than anyone else and he went about the village with a smile on his face

One day, though, as he sat in the tall grass by the river, he heard a group of three young women approaching. They were going to the river to fetch water and as they filled their containers, they talked about the young men in the village and which one they would like to marry. Because of his shyness, Manyan stayed hidden. Though he was concealed, he could see them and he could hear what they were saying.

"You have mentioned every young man but Manyan," said one young woman. "What about him? He seems like a kind person."

The other two girls began to laugh. "Raven Woman, do you mean that one with the dirty hair and the torn clothes?" said one.

"You would do better to marry a dog," said the other.

But Raven Woman became angry. "You are unkind," she said. "If his hair were combed and his face washed, he would look as good as any of the young men in the village. If I could talk to him, I would tell him what to do."

"Do you wish to have him for a husband?"

"I pity him," Raven Woman said. "If he asked me I would marry him and then I would help him become a man."

The young women filled their containers with water and walked back up the bank, but Manyan stayed hidden in the tall grass for a long time, thinking. At last he arose, went down to the water and washed himself and combed out his hair. Then he sat and waited by the path to the river. When evening came, Raven Woman came again to get water and Manyan stopped her. She looked at him in surprise. With clean face and combed hair, he was more handsome than any of the other young men.

But before she could say anything, he spoke. "I heard your kind words," he said. "I am going to go away to earn a good name. Will you pray to the sun to help me?"

"I will do so," Raven Woman said.

"If I succeed, will you marry me when I return?"

"I will do so gladly."

When the sun rose the next day, Manyan left the camp. He did not know where he would go or what he would do, but he prayed to the sun for help and walked toward the west. It was the time when the nights were cold and the days were growing short. He had very little food with him and his bow and arrows were too poor to kill anything, but he continued on his way.

Manyan walked for many days until he came to the top of a hill overlooking a valley. Below was a huge beaver dam with a great pond behind it. The grass growing in the meadow next to the pond was tall and dry and Manyan pulled armloads of it to make himself a bed for the night. But just as he was ready to sleep, someone called his name.

He looked up and saw in front of him a handsome young man in beautiful fur clothing. "Manyan," the young man said, "you look cold and tired. My father's lodge is nearby and he wants you to be his guest."

"I didn't see your father's lodge when I looked down on this valley from the hilltop," Manyan said.

"It is very close," said the young man. "Come with me."

Then the young man led the way out across the ice of the pond and Manyan followed. When they came to the place where the ice ended, there was a very big beaver dam.

"Now you must do as I do," said the young man. "Do not be afraid. Just close your eyes, then dive in and swim."

With that, he dove into the water. Praying for help from the sun, Manyan closed his eyes and dove in after him. To his surprise, the water did not seem cold and after swimming only a short distance, he no longer felt the water around him and he felt something solid under his feet. He opened his eyes and saw that he was inside a great round lodge. In the middle of the lodge was a pool of water whirling around. In the center of that whirlpool a peeled stick floated. Along the walls of the lodge were beds made of robes. A kind-looking old man and his wife sat on one of those beds. On two of the others sat the young man who had guided Manyan and a boy who looked to be his guide's brother. All of them wore beautiful clothing made of fur, but when Manyan looked closer he now saw that these people who looked like humans had fur all over their bodies, even on their faces.

"You are welcome, my son," said the old man. "I am Beaver Chief and this is my lodge. My son saw you in your nest of grass. The nights are too cold for you to sleep without shelter."

"Are you hungry?" said the old woman. "You look thin."

"Of course he is hungry," said Beaver Chief. "We must make him some food."

The old man took a bowl and placed in it some buffalo chips. He broke them up and sang a song over them and they turned into pemmican. Then he gave the bowl to Manyan. Manyan tasted it and was surprised. The food was good.

"Our food is the bark of trees," said Beaver Chief, "but we have learned a great deal through praying and looking for medicines. So we are able to provide you with the food you need. Stay with us and you may learn some things which will be useful.

Look around you. See all that we have gathered."

Manyan looked. The walls of the lodge were all lined with bags and beaded pouches holding medicines, more than he could count.

"I will stay for a while," Manyan said. "Thank you for your generosity."

So Manyan stayed with the beaver people. There was no fire in their lodge, but it was always warm enough and there was plenty of light to see. Whenever one of them left the lodge they would dive into the whirling pool and when they returned, the pool would lift them gently out of the water onto the floor of the lodge. When they ate, they threw the stripped branches into the whirlpool, and it carried them away. But that one stick which Manyan had first seen when he came to Beaver Chief's lodge was always there in the center of the whirlpool.

Winter came and the ice of the pond was all frozen. Now the beaver people spent all of their time in the lodge. They were gentle people and would spend the days praying to their medicines and singing sacred songs. Manyan watched and listened and learned more every day.

At last a day came when the water in the whirling pool turned brown. Beaver Chief's two sons dove in and were gone a long time. When they came back, they had freshly cut alder sticks in their hands.

"The winter is over," they said. "Spring has returned and the ice has broken. Come and see, father!"

While Beaver Chief and his sons were gone, the old woman spoke to Manyan. "My son," she said, "it is almost time for you to leave us. Before you go, my husband will offer you a present. He will say you can choose anything you want in our lodge. The medicine bags on these walls are wonderful things, but you should not choose any of them. Instead, choose that stick there in the center of the pool. It is the most powerful thing we own and it will always help you."

Soon Beaver Chief and his sons returned.

"Spring has come," he said to Manyan. "Now you can return to your people. I am going to give you something to take with you. Look around, see all these medicines. You may choose whatever one you want."

"I will take that stick floating there in the pool," said Manyan.

"Ooo-eee-aii," said Beaver Chief. "What? That old stick there? Surely you want something better. Look at this beautiful pouch here."

"No," said Manyan, "I have chosen. I want only the floating stick."

"My son, my son," said Beaver Chief, quickly leading the young man over to the wall, "look at this beadwork. This is powerful medicine here."

"It is beautiful, indeed," Manyan said, "but I want only that stick."

"Listen to me," Beaver Chief said, "I will tell you what each of these medicines can do. Then you will see that you should choose one of them."

Slowly and carefully, the old man explained each of the medicines and Manyan wondered if his choice had been right, but when he looked at Beaver Chief's wife, she pointed with her lips at the stick in the pool.

"You are kind to tell me all of this," said Manyan, "but my choice has been made. I choose the floating stick."

"Oooo-ee-aii," Beaver Chief said. "You have asked four times for the stick and so I cannot refuse you. You may have it. It is yours. It is the most powerful of all our medicines. When you are in need, it will transform itself into a beaver and help you." Then Beaver Chief reached into the water and the stick swam over to his hand. He tied a string around it and placed it around the young man's neck.

"Now," Beaver Chief said, "follow us." And he and his family dove into the pool.

Manyan followed the beaver people into the pool. He swam a few strokes and found himself standing on the shore. The grass was green and birds sang all around them. It was the height of spring.

"Keep the Beaver Stick under your robe," said Beaver Chief. "Never let anyone see it. When you leave here, remember us but do not look back or the Beaver Stick will leave you." Then Beaver Chief, his wife and two sons dove into the pond and disappeared.

Manyan walked up the hill. His eyes filled with tears as he thought of the kindness of the beaver people. It was hard not to look back at the place where he had spent the winter with his friends but he remembered the old man's words and continued on out of the valley.

He walked until he came to a swift running river, swollen from spring rains. There was no way he could cross and the current was too swift to swim. He took out the Beaver Stick and placed it in the water where it became a beaver.

"My friend," Manyan said, "make a raft for me."

Immediately the beaver cut trees and fastened them together into a strong raft. Then, with Manyan aboard, it pushed the raft across the river. When he reached the other side, Manyan held out his hand and the beaver again became the stick which Manyan hung once more about his neck.

Manyan continued on his way toward the east. Each problem that confronted him as he traveled was solved with the help of the Beaver Stick. At last he came to the hill above the camp of his people and he sat down there on the hilltop in plain sight. Soon some young men came up the hill to see who this stranger was. Manyan covered his face with his robe, for like his friends the beaver people, his body was now covered with fur.

The young men came close, marveling at this stranger's beautiful robe.

"Who are you?" they asked.

"I am Manyan," he said. "I have returned with powerful medicine, but I cannot come into the camp until you do as I tell you. You must build four sweat lodges down by the stream. When they are built and the fire is heating the stones, come and bring me to the first lodge."

The young men recognized by his voice that Manyan was changed and that his power was now great. They went and built the four sweat lodges and returned to the hilltop.

"Walk ahead of me," Manyan said. "Clear away the people and keep them from me as I walk to the sweat lodge."

The young men did as he said. People gathered on all sides as Manyan came down the hill, but none of them came close. He went into the first sweat lodge and the flap was closed behind him. Soon the people heard the sound of water on the stones and the singing of sacred songs. When Manyan left this first lodge, he left behind him a pile of the fur which he had grown during the winter in the beaver lodge.

Into the second lodge he went and again the people heard the hissing of steam and the singing of powerful songs. Again he left behind him a pile of fur as he went into the third lodge and then the fourth. When the fourth sweat was completed, Manyan came out of the lodge dressed in new robes. His face shone and people looked at this tall, strong young man with admiration. Among those who looked at him was Raven Woman. Manyan went to her and took her hand. Neither of them could speak. Her father placed his hands on their shoulders. "That lodge there is yours," said Raven Woman's father. "May your lives together be long and happy."

With the medicine he had learned from the beaver people, Manyan was now able to cure those who were ill. And with the Beaver Stick to help him, he became known as a great warrior, one who could never be defeated as long as water was close at hand. In time, Manyan became a chief of his people. And he and his wife, Raven Woman, did, indeed, lead long and happy lives together.

Chiloquin s Sweat
(Klamath)

There was a man named Chiloquin. He was short, but he was very powerful and tough. Many stories were told about how hardy Chiloquin was.

Once, a group of people were camping in the deep snows on top of the Cascade Mountains when Chiloquin came up on them and said he would spend the night. All he had with him was a thin blanket so he slept beside the fire. When the people woke next morning, there was Chiloquin covered with frost. But when Chiloquin woke up, it seemed he had not suffered. "It was a cool night," Chiloquin said. "I slept well."

A group of Klamaths, Chiloquin among them, went to visit some of the people to the north. While they were visiting, a group of northern shamans decided to go into a sweat lodge to test their power.

"Do you Klamaths have a shaman among you who can accompany us in the sweat lodge?" the northern shamans asked.

"No," the Klamaths said, "but here is Chiloquin. He is not a shaman, but he is pretty tough. He will go with you into the sweat lodge."

So all of the shamans and Chiloquin went into the sweat lodge. Many hot stones were brought in and the lodge flap was closed. Then, one after another, the shamans began to sing their songs and sprinkle water on the hot rocks. The stones hissed and sang as steam filled the lodge.

"Let these stones be hot," the northern shamans sang. "Let the lodge be red hot, let the lodge be white hot."

Each one asked the sweat lodge to grow hotter and hotter. Each one hoped to force the others out with his power. First one shaman and then another was overcome by the heat and had to be dragged out. Finally, the last of the shamans could stand the heat no longer and had to be dragged from the lodge.

But then, outside the lodge, when they had all recovered

enough, the northern shamans looked around. Where was that short Klamath man, that one called Chiloquin? He was nowhere to be seen.

"Is he still in the lodge?" said one northern shaman

"Perhaps he has died," another of the northern shamans said.

Then they heard Chiloquin's voice. Inside the lodge he was talking and throwing even more water on the stones. He continued talking and pouring water for a long time. Finally, when he was ready, he called to them to open the door. Then Chiloquin came out. The shamans had been dragged out, too weak to stand, but Chiloquin stood right up.

"The lodge was warm," he said as he went over to his own people. "That was a pleasant sweat."

Karok old men sunning on stone platform

The Sweat Lodge Without a Bucket
(Watlala)

Three men were ready to do a sweat together. They had made their sweat lodge by the lake and built their fire. Now the stones were heated and ready to be taken into the lodge, but they discovered that they had forgotten one thing. None of the men had brought a bucket to carry water into the lodge and the lake was some distance away from their houses. By the time someone went to get a bucket, the rocks would be too cool.

"I will use my power," the first man said.

He went down to the lake and found a fish carrying basket. The weave of the basket was so loose you could stick your fingers through it, but when he dipped that basket in the water and carried it back to the sweat lodge, not one drop of water leaked out. He put the basket down by the door of the lodge. "Is this not good?" he said.

"That is good," said the second man. "Now let me see what I can do with my power."

He, too, went down to the lake and found there a dip-net. He put the dip-net into the lake and it came up filled. He carried it back up to the sweat lodge and the net did not leak out even one drop of water when he placed it down beside the first man's basket. "Is this not even better?" the second man said.

"I, too, will bring back some water," said the third man, who had remained silent until then.

He walked down to the lake, knelt, put his hands into the water and moved them in a circle. When he stood up, he was holding a ball of water, twice the size of a man's head. He carried it back to the lodge and placed it on the ground next to the basket and the net. When he poked his finger into it, water ran out.

"This may not be good enough," the third man said. "It leaks too easily."

The other two men said nothing, but when they went into the lodge, the third man was the one who led the sweat.

Sweat lodge with buffalo skull, sage and forked sticks

WHEN TRICKSTER ENTERS THE LODGE

When Trickster Enters the Lodge

One of the primary figures in Native stories is Trickster. As full of appetite and contradictory impulses as we humans are, Trickster is often the most perfect example of what not to do. Ruled by appetite and selfishness, Trickster is not only laughable, he is also a very dangerous being. Anyone who listens to him invariably gets into trouble. If it were not for the fact that Trickster deceives himself even more easily than he deceives others, he would be even more threatening and, probably, much less popular and useful as a character in lesson stories.

Virtually every Native culture in North America has its own cycle of Trickster tales. Sometimes male, sometimes female, or even playing both roles—as in the story of how Coyote imitates a woman and marries a chief's son so that he can eat the whole marriage feast—Trickster may be a coyote, a spider, a raven, a hare, a wolverine, a fox, or a human being. Whatever and wherever he or she is, Trickster almost always is the embodiment of a negative example. If there is a right way to do things, Trickster will do the opposite—and the sweat lodge is no exception.

In every sweat lodge ceremony I know, one is supposed to fast before the sweat and the idea of eating while in the lodge itself is out of the question. Yet in the Yakima tale from the Pacific northwest of Coyote and Deer Man, we see Coyote in a lodge whose poles are deer ribs, licking up the deer fat which drips down onto him. The sweat lodge is universally seen as a place for cleansing, purification and healing. Yet Wolverine, in the Passamaquoddy story from the Atlantic northeast, has no compunctions about using it as a way to deceive Bear and lead him to his doom.

One of the reasons, I've been told, why you should always know the people with whom you go into a sweat lodge is that a stranger might actually be Trickster in disguise. And when Trickster enters the lodge, it is the right time for everyone else to leave it.

Wolverine and Bear
(Passamaquoddy)

Long ago, Lahks, the wolverine, was out walking around. It had been some time since he had eaten and he was very hungry. As he walked, he came upon Mooin, the bear.

"Let us sit on this log and smoke our pipes together," Wolverine said and Bear agreed.

But as they sat there, Ka-ahk, the gull, flew overhead. Wolverine had just come from the cliffs by the bay where Gull lived. Wolverine had tried to climb up to where the gulls laid their eggs but the gulls had flown down in a great flock to drive him away before he reached their nests. As Wolverine and Bear sat on the log smoking their pipes, Gull flew down close to them and then— FWOP! A big splatter of gull droppings landed right on Wolverine's head.

"Arrrhh," Wolverine growled, as he wiped off the bird droppings, "Gull is very ungrateful. How could he do this to me after I used my magic to turn him white?"

"Was not Gull always white?" Bear said.

"Hurnnnh," Wolverine growled, "he was as black as Gahgah, the Crow, before I took him into my lodge and purified him. You know that I am a great motewolon, a powerful doctor. But why do you ask me this?"

Now Wolverine, of course, was not telling the truth. Gull had always been white. And Wolverine also already knew why Bear was asking him that question. Everyone knew that Bear, whose coat was all black—except for one little spot high on his chest that he could not see—wanted very much to be as white as his powerful cousins to the north.

"My friend," Bear said, "can you make me white?"

"I could do so," said Wolverine, "but it is hard. I think you are not strong enough to stand it."

Now Bear was very proud of his strength. He did not like those words. "I am strong enough to stand anything," Bear said.

"Take me to your lodge and turn me white."

So Wolverine led Bear down close to the shore. There he made a small round lodge of saplings which he wove together. He piled stones around the base and then covered the whole lodge with moss and seaweeds. Then he made a fire and heated a great pile of round stones in it. When all was ready, he put Bear into the lodge. He picked up red-hot stones with green forked sticks and placed many of them in the center of the lodge. Then Wolverine went out and shut the door.

"Are you not coming inside?" Bear said.

"No," Wolverine said. "I do not want to turn white. And you are very large. I must use all of my power to make you change color."

Then, through a small hole in the roof of the sweat lodge, Wolverine began to pour in water. Steam filled the lodge and hissed out through the hole in the roof.

The lodge grew hotter and hotter and Bear roared.

"Oooo-oooh! It is too hot! I am dying."

"Hunrrh," Wolverine growled, "I knew you were not strong enough to do this. It was twice as hot as this when I purified Gull. I have just started."

At that, Bear stopped moaning. Then he said. "I am strong enough. Continue."

Wolverine poured more water in through the roof. It became so hot in the lodge that Bear could stand it no longer. He pushed his way out through the door and collapsed on the sand.

"Look," Bear said, holding his paws in front of his face, 'your medicine has not worked, I am still not white."

"Arrhhh," Wolverine growled. "I have not yet finished my work. If you had remained inside you would have turned all white. My medicine was just starting to work. Already your chest was beginning to turn white."

Bear looked down but could not see that white spot on his chest which had, of course, always been there. Then Wolverine led him down to the water and had him look at his reflection. Bear was pleased to see that white spot on his chest. It seemed to him that Wolverine's medicine had started to work.

"You see," Wolverine said, "you were beginning to turn white, but you stopped too soon."

"I will go in again," Bear said. "This time I will not stop."

So Bear went back into the lodge. Wolverine put in more red-hot stones, closed the door and poured water in through the hole on top. The steam rose from the stones and it grew even hotter than before. Bear moaned, but he wanted to turn white and so he did not come out. He did not come out when it grew so hot he could hardly breathe.

"Bear," Wolverine said, "is it too hot for you?"

But Bear did not answer. It had become so hot in the lodge that he had died.

Then Wolverine opened up the lodge. Now he would no longer be hungry. He would have enough bear meat to eat for a long time.

How Coyote Made the Seasons
(Nez Perce)

In the old days, Sun shone hot all of the time. It was always summer and it was always so hot that the earth became dry and the people were unhappy.

"I can do something about this," Coyote said. 'I can take the place of Sun." He went to the highest hill and called Sun, asking him to come down, but Sun paid no attention and just went by toward the west. Coyote jumped as high as he could, but he could not reach the sun. He ran to the place where Sun was low in the sky, but he could not catch him. Sun always stayed ahead of Coyote, high up in the sky.

Finally Coyote asked Frog to help him.

"I will throw you up in the sky," Coyote said. "Your hands are sticky and you can hold on to Sun and bring him down."

"That is a good plan," Frog said. "I will do it."

Then Coyote and Frog climbed up the mountain and waited till Sun was passing over them. Coyote threw Frog as hard as he could at Sun. Then, knowing that Frog would have a long journey before he was able to bring Sun back to earth, Coyote went down the mountain to make ready for Sun's arrival.

First Coyote used his power to make a campfire. As soon as the campfire was burned down, he covered it with dirt. Then he set up some old lodge poles for a tipi, but he did not cover them. Last of all, he took willows and made a framework for a sweat lodge beside the river. Using his power, he made the willow frame look like it had stood there for a long time.

When Frog returned with Sun, Coyote was ready.

"My friend," Coyote said to Sun, "I am glad you have come to visit. Our fathers were good friends. Let me show you the place where they used to camp together. Then Coyote showed Sun the worn tipi poles.

"That is where their tipi stood," Coyote said.

"I see," Sun said.

Coyote scraped away the earth covering the campfire. "Here are the remains of the last fire they shared together."

"I see," Sun said. It was clear to him now that his father and Coyote's father must have known each other long ago.

Then Coyote showed Sun the framework of the sweat lodge. "Here is the place where our fathers had their sweat lodge."

"Ah," Sun said, "they must have been good friends."

"That is why you and I must be friends now," Coyote said. "Let us camp here together."

And so Sun agreed to camp with Coyote. They spent the day together hunting and when night came they made camp and lay down to rest. Coyote waited until he was certain Sun was asleep and crept over toward Sun, his flint knife in his hand. He was planning to kill Sun and take his place, but Sun's eyes were still wide open.

"What is wrong, my friend?" Sun asked. "Why do you have your knife in your hand?"

"My friend," Coyote said, "I am hungry. I am just going to cut myself a piece of meat from that deer haunch we hung on the tree branch."

"That is a good idea, my friend," Sun said. "If you are hungry, you should eat."

"My friend," Coyote said, "are you not going to close your eyes and sleep?"

"I never close my eyes," Sun said.

Now Coyote did not know what to do. If Sun always slept with his eyes open, it seemed there would be no way Coyote could kill him. But each night, Coyote made his bed a little closer to Sun. Finally, on the fifth night, Coyote went to bed with his flint knife in his hand. He waited until the middle of the night and then he spoke. "My friend," Coyote said to the Sun, "what is that strange animal over there?"

When Sun turned to look, Coyote pulled out his flint knife and cut off Sun's head.

Now Coyote could be the sun. By killing Sun, he had taken his power and it was easy for him to go up into the sky. Day after day, Coyote was the sun going over the earth. At first it was interesting, for he could see all the things that all the people below were doing, even when they thought no one was watching. But, after a time. Coyote grew bored with doing the same thing every day. "This work is too hard," Coyote said. "I must bring Sun back to life."

Coyote went down to earth and made the sweat lodge ready. He dragged Sun's body into the sweat lodge and placed Sun's head back on his shoulders. Then he began to heat the lodge. When the lodge was very hot, Coyote jumped back and forth over Sun's body four times. As soon as Coyote had jumped the fourth time, Sun sat up, alive and well.

"My rest was good," Sun said. "I was tired from working so hard."

"That is true," Coyote said. "You have been working too hard. So this is what you must do from this day on. You will not work as hard as you used to work, making the earth hot. From now on there will be seasons. There will be a hot season when the sun shines much of the day. That will be summer. Then there will be a medium time when you start to rest. That time will be autumn. The season when you rest the most will be cold. That time will be winter. Then there will be another time in between winter and summer when you start to work a little harder each day. That time will be spring. Those will be the four parts of the year from now on.

And because Sun agreed with Coyote's idea, we have those four seasons today.

Coyote and Deer Spirit
(Yakima)

One day Coyote was walking along. He had been hunting, but all he was able to catch and kill were two young deer. He was carrying them home, and as he walked along, he came to the place where Deer Man and his wife lived.

"I think I will go visit these old people," Coyote said. He threw down the two young deer, dropped his bow and arrows, and entered Deer Man's lodge. It was a good lodge. The poles of the lodge were covered with deer skins and deer meat hung all around the lodge. Coyote saw that Deer Man's lodge was a very good lodge, indeed, and he began to feel hungry.

"Speel-yi, you are welcome," Deer Man said. "I am about to do a sweat. Come and join me in my whe-a'cht."

When they went inside the whe-a'cht, Coyote saw that sweat lodge was very good. The framework of the lodge was not made of poles. It was made of big deer ribs! The lodge was very hot from the stones and when Deer Man poured water on the rocks, fat began to drip down on Coyote from the deer ribs. Coyote licked the fat off himself. He was getting hungrier.

'Be patient, Speel-yi," Deer Man said when he saw Coyote licking that deer fat. "Do not eat now. We will have a big feast when we are through with the sweat."

At last, when they had done five rounds, the sweat was over. Then Deer Man called for the door to be opened. "Who-o-ooah!" he shouted.

Then a young deer came and opened the deerskin door-covering. As they came out, Coyote thought to himself, "I will kill Deer Man. Then I will have his lodge and everything that is in it. I'll have this fine sweat lodge and all this meat."

But when Coyote grabbed Deer Man, Deer Man knew what Coyote intended to do. "Too-o-o tah-ni-tic," he called out to the others. "Run away, all of you!"

"It will do you no good to call your Too-tah," Coyote said.

91

"Your papa will not help you."

Then Coyote threw Deer Man onto a big stone which had small holes in it. He picked up another rock to beat Deer Man with, but Deer Man was quick and his power was great. He made himself very small and escaped into one of the holes in the rock. Coyote did not even notice. He pounded and pounded on the big stone with the rock. When he stopped, he looked around.

"Ah," Coyote said, "I have beaten him so hard that there is nothing of him left!"

He turned around and what should he see but the two little deer he had killed and dropped by the entrance to Deer Man's lodge. One of those dead deer was standing up. "Where are you going?" Coyote said. "I have already killed you."

But as he watched, the second little deer stood up, too, and then both of them ran away. Coyote turned around. The sweat lodge was gone and so was Deer Man's lodge with all of that good deer meat. Coyote walked over to his bow and arrows and picked them up. The deer sinew string of his bow had disappeared and the points all fell off the arrows because the sinew which had tied them on was also gone. Then Coyote noticed that he was naked. His fine deerskin shirt, his deerskin leggings, and all his clothing had vanished.

"I do not understand this," Coyote said. "I killed Deer Man and now his lodge is gone, his whe-a'cht is gone, and all that good deer meat is gone. Everything of deer has disappeared."

Then Coyote went home. When he came to his lodge, he saw a strange sight. All that was left were the wooden poles. His wife stood there with nothing on. All her fine deerskin clothes had vanished, too.

"Speel-yi," she said, "what have you done now? You have done something bad and my clothes have left me. Where is the food you were going to bring home?"

"I went to the lodge of Deer Man," Coyote said. "His lodge was full of meat. He had a fine sweat house with deer meat hanging in it. I thought that if I killed him everything he had would be ours."

"Speel-yi," Coyote's wife said. "Deer Man is the owner of all the deer and everything that is made from the deer. Now that you have treated him that way, we have lost everything. We have no lodge. We no longer have clothes to wear. You can no longer use your bow and arrows."

"I know that," said Coyote.

So, ever since then, Coyote and his wife and all his people have had to live without lodges and clothes and bows and arrows. It is still that way to this day.

Coyote and Gray Giant
(Dineh [Navajo])

Coyote asked a young woman to marry him. "I cannot marry you," she said.

"Why is that?" Coyote asked.

"I can only marry someone who has destroyed one of Naayee', the monsters that prey on the people," she said.

"I can do that," said Coyote. Then he set off for the hogan of Gray Giant.

Gray Giant was one of those monsters that killed and ate the people. He was half the height of a tall pine tree and he liked nothing better than preying on the human beings.

But Coyote came right up to him and greeted him. "Big brother,' Coyote said, "I have come here to help you. I know that you enjoy hunting the human beings, but you are not always able to catch them because you are not fast enough."

"That is true," Gray Giant rumbled. "The little ones are good to eat, but they are very quick."

"Look at me," Coyote said, 'I am very fast. I am fast enough to outrun the mountain lion. I can catch anything that I want to eat, so I am never hungry. Would you like to know how I made myself so fast."

"Little brother," Gray Giant said, "I am always hungry. I would like to know how to become as fast as you."

"Good," Coyote said, "I will show you what to do so you will no longer be hungry. We will have a sweat together. I will go and get the blankets to cover the doorway. You build the sweat house and then gather wood and make a fire."

While Gray Giant was working, Coyote went to the place where he had seen his cousin Wolf kill a deer some time ago. All that was left of that deer were some of the long bones. Coyote selected one which was just the size of one of his own thighbones. Then, hiding the bones under his blankets, Coyote went back to Gray Giant's hogan.

By the time he returned, Gray Giant had built the sweat house and a great fire made of tree trunks was roaring in front of it. Coyote placed some big stones into the fire and then used his four blankets to cover the door of the house. He put on the white blanket, the blue blanket, the yellow blanket, and the black blanket and he saw that they covered the door very well. It would be completely dark inside the lodge and that was important for Coyote's plan to work.

"Now I have to make it ready for us inside the sweat house," Coyote said to Gray Giant. "Wait outside until I am ready."

Coyote went into the sweat house to put down cedar boughs on the floor of the lodge around the hole for the hot stones. While he was in there he hid that deer thighbone close to the place where he would sit. Then Coyote came out. The stones were very hot now and Coyote carried them into the sweat house and placed them in the hole in the center.

"Now everything is ready," Coyote said. "Now we must go into the sweat house."

"That is good," Gray Giant said. "I am very hungry and when I become fast I will be able to catch and eat many people.

Coyote and Gray Giant took off all their clothes and crawled into the sweat house, taking nothing with them except a very large flint knife which Coyote carried. They pulled the blanket over the opening and now, except for the glowing of the stones, all was dark.

"I am going to show you how to make yourself a fast runner," Coyote said. "You saw the flint knife I brought into this sweat house with me. Every time you want to make yourself faster, you must make a sweat house. When you go inside, you must take this flint knife with you and use it to cut away all of the flesh from your thigh. It will hurt, but you must do it to make yourself faster. After you have done that, you must break the bone. As soon as you do that, the broken bone will heal back together and new flesh will grow. Now, to show you how to do it, I will go first."

Then, in the dark of the sweat house, Coyote pretended to cut the flesh off his leg. He moaned and cried as he did so. Then he took the deer thighbone and placed it on top of his outstretched leg.

"Big brother," Coyote groaned, "it is very painful, but I have done it. All the flesh is cut away from my thigh. Reach over and you can feel the bone of my leg.

Gray Giant reached over and felt the deer bone. "Little brother," Gray Giant said, "I feel the bone of your leg. But doesn't it hurt."

"It hurts very much," Coyote said, "but the more it hurts, the faster you become. Now I must break the bone."

Then Coyote struck the stone knife against the deer bone—whack! whack! whack! whack!—until it finally broke.

"Big brother," Coyote groaned, "feel how my thigh bone is broken? Now move your hand back and I will make it heal."

Then Coyote hid the deer bone under the cedar boughs again and began to sing and pray very loudly.

"It is healing," Coyote chanted, "it is healing, it is healing, the pain is going, the pain is gone." At last Coyote told Gray Giant to feel his leg again.

"It is healed," Gray Giant said.

"That is true, cousin," Coyote said. "My leg is stronger than before and I am faster than I was. Now it is your turn. Do just as I told you and soon you will no longer be hungry."

Gray Giant eagerly took Coyote's stone knife and began to cut the flesh from his thigh. "Ahhhh," Gray Giant moaned, "it is very painful. It hurts so much that I am sure I am going to be very fast." He continued cutting, crying with pain as he did so, until he had cut away the flesh from his thighbone just as he thought Coyote had done.

"I have cut away the flesh," Gray Giant groaned. "Now what must I do?"

"Do you not remember?" Coyote said. 'Quick, break the bone. Then your suffering will soon be over and you will be hungry no longer."

Gray Giant took the knife and struck his thigh bone—whack! whack! whack! whack!—until the bone broke.

"It is healing, it is healing," Gray Giant chanted, but the wound did not heal.

"Little Brother," Gray Giant groaned, "it is not healing. Tell me what I have done wrong. Help me to heal my leg."

'Can you stand and walk?" Coyote said.

"I am too weak to move," said Gray Giant."

"Then your suffering is almost over," Coyote said. "Soon you will be hungry no longer."

Then Coyote went outside and got his bow and arrows. He came back into the sweat house and shot all of his arrows into Gray Giant.

So Coyote did as he said he would do. Coyote killed one of the monsters that preyed on the human beings long ago.

Coyote and the Navajo
(Hopi)

Haliksa'i. This is my story. Coyote was living with his old grandmother. Coyote was not a very good hunter. Sometimes he would bring home a lizard and some other small animal, but he was not fast enough to catch bigger things and so they often went hungry.

One day, though, Coyote went over near Oraivi. There were Hopi people there and not far from the village was a flock of sheep. Coyote crept down, grabbed one of those sheep and carried it home to his grandmother. Then they ate well. A few days later, Coyote went back and stole another sheep. Coyote was very proud of himself. He had learned how to bring home plenty of food and this went on for a little while, but the Hopi men who were caring for the flock saw that their sheep were vanishing.

"It is that Coyote we have been seeing," the Hopi men said.

So they put the sheep into a pen and kept watch over them. The next time Coyote came, the man who was guarding the sheep shouted at Coyote and threw stones at him. Coyote was very frightened and ran away.

Coyote had to find food somewhere else. He roamed all around and finally found another herd of sheep far to the east of Oraivi. These sheep were owned by a Navajo family and the only people guarding them were two small boys. He waited until it was dark and the sheep were in their corral. Then he sneaked down, grabbed one, and carried it back home to his grandmother. Now Coyote was happy. Whenever he was hungry, he would sneak back to that place and steal another sheep from the Navajos.

But the father of those boys soon noticed that his sheep were disappearing. He had seen Coyote hanging around and knew that he was the one taking those sheep.

One day, Coyote got up very early because he was hungry.

"I am going hunting," he said to his grandmother and then he set out for the place where the Navajos had their herd of sheep. He left so early that it was the middle of the day when he got there, and he settled down on the hill above the camp to watch. The first thing he saw was something new. There was a very small hogan built down there near the corral. It was shaped like a beehive made of wood and covered with mud and straw, with blankets over the top and a blanket over the door. A fire was burning next to that hogan and smoke seemed to be coming from the hogan itself. Coyote became very curious.

"I wonder what that is down there?" he said to himself. "I could go and ask whoever is inside. But maybe they don't speak Hopi and they wouldn't understand me."

Finally, Coyote got so curious he just had to see. He started down the hill, and just as he was about to reach the lodge a Navajo man came out. Coyote got ready to run away, but the man paid no attention to him. The Navajo man was all covered with sweat and he began to throw sand on his body to dry himself off.

Coyote trotted up to him. "What are you doing?" Coyote said.

To his surprise, the Navajo man understood him and answered him in Hopi. "This is my sweat bath," the man said. "I take a sweat every day to make myself clean. Whenever I take a sweat, it makes me a faster runner, too. I can run as long as I want without tiring after taking a sweat bath."

That sounded good to Coyote. "If I do this thing," he thought, "it will make me so fast that when I come out I can grab a sheep and run away without being caught."

So Coyote said to the man, "Can I take a sweat bath?"

"Perhaps you can," said the man. "First I must heat up more stones and make the sweat house ready for you. When the stones are hot, you can go inside. I'll pour the water on the stones for you to make the steam and then I'll leave you in there by yourself so you can have a really good sweat bath. I'll close the door up real tight so none of that steam can get out and I'll open the door up later."

That, too, sounded good to Coyote and he sat down to wait.

The Navajo man built up the fire and put in more stones. Then he went over and picked up a big armful of dry cedar bark. "I will put this on the floor of the lodge to make it better for you," he said to Coyote. Then he covered the floor of the sweat house with the cedar bark. By the time he was finished, the stones were glowing red. The Navajo man moved the red-hot stones into the center of his sweat house and then told Coyote to go inside.

"Sit at the back of the hogan and face the wall," he said to Coyote. "Then the steam won't burn your eyes. As soon as I pour on the water, I'm going to close the door."

"That's good," Coyote said. "Just be sure to open the door when it is time for me to come out."

"Don't worry," said the Navajo man, holding up the dipper in his right hand. "Now close your eyes because I am going to pour on the water."

As the water hit the hot stones, steam filled the sweat house, just as the Navajo man said it would. Coyote kept his eyes shut tight and faced the wall as he had been told. So he did not see that the Navajo man had a burning stick in his left hand. He touched that stick to the dry cedar bark and blew on it, setting the floor of the hogan on fire. Then, before Coyote saw that anything was wrong, the Navajo man closed the door of the sweat house, rolled a big stone over the door, and propped a log against that stone to hold it in place.

Inside the lodge, Coyote was getting hot. "I am going to be a very fast runner when I come out of here," Coyote said. "I will be very fast indeed!"

Now, however, the smoke from the burning cedar was making it hard for Coyote to breathe. "I think I am hot enough," Coyote said. "This is a very good sweat house, but I am ready to come out."

The Navajo man did not answer him, for he had already ridden away.

"I do not want to be too fast," Coyote shouted. "You must

open the door now."

When there was no answer, Coyote jumped up, hitting his head on the roof of the sweat house. He went to the door, but he could not open it. The smoke grew thicker and thicker and finally Coyote died.

Later, the Navajo man came back and took Coyote's body up into the hills and left it there. When Coyote came back to life again, he stood up and shook his legs.

"That sweat house was no good," Coyote said. "I do not think it has made me faster."

And, ever since then, Coyote has never gone into a sweat house again.

Medicine sweat tipi

A Dog for the Sweat Lodge
(Cheyenne)

It is traditional among the Cheyenne for a young man who wants to do a special sweat to bring a young dog with him as an offering. That dog will be eaten in the meal after the sweat. Knowing that may help you understand this story which was given to me by Lance Henson, a Cheyenne poet who is a member of the Dog Soldier Society. Lance and I had just finished doing a winter sweat together. As we sat around eating dinner he laughed and said, "Here's a sweat lodge story that you can put into your book."

Not too long ago, two young Cheyenne men asked one of their elders to put on a sweat for them.

"Because you have asked me," he said, "I will do this for you. But you remember what you have to bring."

Those two young men were really excited. They could hardly wait for that day. But when the day came and they were on their way there, one of them looked at the other and said, "Did you bring the puppy?"

"No, didn't you bring it?"

Now they were stuck. They knew that if they didn't show up with a puppy, that old man would never agree to do the sweat for them. But as they were driving along, there sitting on a porch by the roadside was a puppy, wagging its tail back and forth.

"You thinking what I'm thinking?" the first young man asked.

So they stopped the car, got out and went up to the porch. Nobody was around but that puppy that kept looking up at them and wagging its tail. So they picked it up and got back in their pickup.

When they got to the place where the sweat was going to be done, they brought that puppy to the old man. "This is a good dog. You have done well," he said. "Now you have to prepare it."

Well, those two young men looked at each other again. That puppy was so cute that neither one of them wanted to be the one to do it. It just sat there wagging its tail back and forth.

"Go on," said the first young man.

'No, you do it," said the second one.

They argued back and forth until they could see that the old man was about to lose patience with them. "All right," said the first young man, " I'll kill him. You just hold him."

Then, as the second young man held the dog, he took a stick and hit it on the head. It stopped wagging its tail and went limp.

Neither one of them felt good about it, but now that they'd killed it they could get on with their special sweat.

"What do we do now?" they said.

"Take this paint and paint him in the sacred way," the old man said. Then they painted red and black stripes from the dog's head down its back.

"That's good," said the old man. "Now you got to singe his hair off before we cook him."

So they carried the dog's body over to the fire and they rolled him into it. But what they didn't know was that they hadn't really hit that dog hard enough to kill it. As soon as they rolled it into that fire, it woke up with a yelp. It jumped out of that fire and took off across the fields, trailing smoke and setting off little brush fires in its wake. It went so fast that it was out of sight before those two young men could even think about trying to catch it.

"Well," the old man said, "no dog, no sweat. Maybe you can try again in a month or so." And he put out the fire, packed up his things, and left.

Those two young men were really depressed. They got into their pickup and drove back towards home. And on their way, as they went past that house what did they see but that puppy! Its tail singed, red and black stripes down its back, it just sat there as they drove by, wagging its tail back and forth.

THE HEALING LODGE

The Healing Lodge

I have always associated steam with health. Perhaps it is because I have such vivid memories of the vaporizer my grandmother would place by my bed before she would make a tent of a blanket so that I was engulfed by the moist hot steam until the sweat came that broke my fever. According to Virgil J. Vogel in his landmark volume *American Indian Medicine,* that type of steam therapy became popular among white Americans in the United States in the early 1800s. Its popularity was a result of such "empiric practitioners" as Samuel Thompson, an uneducated New England farmer who used steaming and sweating patients to cure a wide variety of ills. But Thompson did not operate in a vacuum, for the practice of steaming and sweating patients for rheumatism, colds, and fevers had long been practiced by the Abenaki Indians, who lived near his farm. It is quite likely that their understanding of the curative powers of steam and sweats was passed on in some way to Thompson and the many others of his era who became known as "Indian doctors."

That understanding of the direct curative power of sweats has been forgotten or neglected by some of the Native nations of North America—so much so that a Mohawk friend of mine went so far as to say that "sweats are not part of my tradition." Yet Annemarie Shimony in her 1961 publication *Conservativism Among the Iroquois at the Six Nations Reserve* relates in some detail the healing sweats that Iroquois described to her as having been done by their own elders. My Creek Indian friend, Louis Littlecoon Oliver, with whom I shared a sweat lodge when he was in his late seventies, took me through the woods around my own home identifying plants common to both the northeast and the southeast which were still used in sweat lodges by his people because of their curative powers when added to the water that is sprinkled on the stones.

Today, in many parts of North America, the healing tradition of the sweat lodge is very much alive and used in a number of ways. The Native approach of healing the whole person—not just alleviating a physical symptom as does Western medicine—is exemplified in the sweat lodge. In alcohol and drug-counseling programs in Saskatchewan, for example, following sessions in which Native elders explain the old ways of being in spiritual, emotional, mental, and physical balance, the sweat lodge is used for holistic healing. The many kinds of healing associated with the sweat, including the restoration of life itself, can be found in the stories in this section. Also, perhaps more than in any other section of this book, the understanding that we human beings are not alone and that animals serve as both teachers and friends worthy of true respect, is expressed here, especially in the Creek story, "The Coming of Medicines."

The fact that the healing power of the sweat lodge is still so important to Native people today is one reason why many Native Americans look unfavorably upon non-Natives who make use of sweat lodges without the kind of respect and guidance that such a powerful gift from the Creator deserves. Sherman Alexie, a wonderfully talented writer, is a Spokane/Coeur D'Alene Indian from Wellpinit, Washington, where the sweat lodge traditions are very much alive. In a sometimes funny, sometimes angry piece entitled "White Men Can't Drum," which appeared in the *New York Times Book Review* in 1992, he criticized the random appropriation of American Indian traditions found in the men's movement and the cavalier use of sweat lodges. "The sweat lodge," Alexie said, "is my church."

First Man and the Cedar Bough Lodge
(Santee Dakota)

The One Who Was First Created lived long ago with his younger brother. They lived close to the great water. One day, as First Man's brother walked alone by the lake, the monsters which lived in its depths grabbed him. They dragged him into the lake and ate him. All that was left of the younger brother of First Man were his bones, and they were at the bottom of the great water.

First Man went into the lake to fight with the water monsters. He defeated them and then dove down deep to gather together the bones of his dead brother. Then, on the shore of the great water, he dug two round holes. He bent together willow poles and tied them together over the first hole and then he covered those poles with cedar boughs, making a small lodge. Within that lodge he placed his younger brother's dry bones. In the second hole he built a fire and in that fire he heated four round stones.

When those stones were very hot, First Man rolled them one by one into the cedar bough lodge. Then, sitting outside the lodge, he began to sing. There was an animal skin filled with water at his side and he held a bunch of sage in his hand. As he sang, he dipped the sage into the water and then thrust his arm into the cedar bough lodge to sprinkle water on the stones. Steam rose and within the darkness of the lodge there was a motion.

First Man continued to sing and sprinkled the stones with the water from the sage. Steam rose again and there was the sound of his brother's bones coming together. A third time he sprinkled water, and as the steam rose he heard the sound of his brother's breath and a soft voice singing with him as he sang.

He reached his arm into the cedar bough lodge and sprinkled water a fourth time and his brother's voice spoke clearly from within the lodge. "Brother, let me out."

So, through First Man's cedar bough lodge, his younger brother was returned to life.

The Coming of Medicines
(Creek)

Long ago, the people offended the animals. When they killed an animal such as a deer, they took only part of the animals and left the rest to spoil. When they caught fish from the streams and the lakes, they threw the bones into the fire or back into the water. They forgot to show gratitude to the animals for agreeing to be killed so that the people could continue to live. They hunted the animals so much that the animals became scarce.

So the animals held a council to decide what they should do. Some wished to go to war with the humans. But the Bear cautioned them. "The human beings now have bows and arrows. They can kill animals at a distance and so we animals are no longer a match for them."

They talked back and forth a long time and at last it was decided. They would send sicknesses to punish the people. The deer sent swollen joints and rheumatic pains and headaches, the birds sent stomach troubles. They sent many problems to the human beings and the humans began to suffer greatly. They suffered so greatly that the animals took pity on them. They spoke to certain humans when they dreamt and told them why their people now had such problems.

Then, through dreams and visions, they sent certain humans remedies for those illnesses. They sent medicine songs and told the humans who would become healers how to use certain plants to cure their illnesses and how to use the sweat lodge.

Now that the sicknesses had been sent to the people, those sicknesses would always be with them. But if the healers, these people who had been given those songs in their dreams and visions, sang the medicine songs which the animals taught them, if they crawled as naked as the animals themselves into the sweat lodge to purify themselves, they would be able to cure the sick. If they imitated the animals which had sent the sicknesses to them and asked those animals for forgiveness, they could make people well again. Then, if those who were cured always remembered to not overhunt; if they treated the remains of the animals they killed in the proper way, those sicknesses would not return to them.

So medicines and the sweat lodge and the healing songs and all the other means to cure illnesses were given to the people. They were given by the same animals who sent sicknesses to punish the people because they had not treated the animals properly.

Stone Boy
(Lakota)

Four brothers lived together with their sister. Each day the brothers would go out hunting, each on his own path. When they came home at night they would share whatever game they brought back with their sister. One day the oldest of the four brothers did not return. The next day, the three remaining brothers went out and when they came back that night one of them was missing. On the next day, the same thing happened. Finally, on the fourth day, only the youngest brother was left.

When he started to go hunting, the sister pleaded with him. "Hakela, youngest brother, do not leave."

But the youngest brother did not listen. He left and he, too, did not come back.

Now the sister did not know what to do. She was so filled with sorrow that she could not eat or drink. All she could do was walk around and cry. Finally, she became so thirsty that she picked up a round shiny pebble and put it in her mouth to suck on it. But as she was carrying the stone in her mouth and weeping, she swallowed it. As soon as she did so, she became pregnant and gave birth to a baby boy.

"I cannot care for you," she said to the baby, and she picked him up and placed him outside the door of her lodge. But as soon as she went back inside, the stone boy came crawling in behind her, the size of a child of two winters. Again she picked him up and placed him outside the lodge. This time he came walking back in, the size of a youth. She picked him up a third time and placed him outside. This time when he came back, the stone boy was a young man, so much larger than his mother that she could not pick him up.

"My son," she said, "you can stay with me, but I wish you had clothing to wear." She looked up at the stone boy. He was now dressed in fine buckskins.

"Ah," the mother said, "I wish that my son had a bow and

111

arrows so that he could use them for hunting." She turned around to look and saw a strong bow and many arrows were now leaning against the side of the tipi. So Stone Boy had all that he needed.

Stone Boy and his mother lived there in the tipi for some time and everything went well. Then one day Stone Boy looked at his mother across the fire and said, "Why do we live alone? Don't we have any relatives?"

"You had four uncles," his mother said. "They went out hunting and never returned."

"Then I shall go find them," Stone Boy said.

"Do not leave me alone," his mother said and she wept for him to stay. But Stone Boy did not listen. He set out on the trail which led away from their tipi toward the north. He traveled for a long time until he came to a small tipi, so old that the skin of the tipi was yellow with age. Four bundles wrapped in skins leaned against the tipi.

A huge old woman came out of the tipi as he approached. "Grandson," she said, "stop and help me. My back is sore, but if you will just walk on it, it will be better. Your uncles helped me by treading on my back before they went on their way."

Stone Boy looked at the huge old woman. He could see that her heart was bad. "This old woman means to kill me," he thought. But he did not let the old woman know what he thought.

"Grandmother," Stone Boy said, "I will do what I can do."

Then he began to walk on the old woman's back, massaging it. But as he walked, he saw that her back bone was sharp. It was so sharp that he knew it would kill him if he fell on it. The huge old woman shook herself, to make Stone Boy fall, but instead he jumped up and came down on her with such force that she was killed.

Then Stone Boy looked at the four bundles leaning against the lodge.

"These are the bodies of my dead uncles," he said. "I will do what I can do to help them."

Stone Boy now heard spirit voices talking to him. "Cut twelve willow poles from beside the stream," the voices said. "Place them in the ground and bend them over to make a shape like a beehive."

Stone Boy cut the willows and did as the voices instructed. He covered the beehive of poles with skins and then placed the four bundles which held the bodies of his uncles inside the small lodge. He heated stones in a fire till they were red hot and then brought them into the lodge. He brought water in an animal skin bag and then closed the doorflap of the lodge so that all was dark inside.

"You have brought me here," he said to the stones and he thanked them. Then he began to pour water on them and sing as the steam rose. After he had poured water four times, other voices joined him. His uncles had come back to life and were singing with him. When the door was opened, he saw his uncles sitting there around the stones, alive and well.

"The stones gave me life," Stone Boy said to his uncles, "and these stones have returned life to you. From this day on, our people will have this inipi, this sweat lodge, to purify them and give them health."

So the first sweat lodge was made.

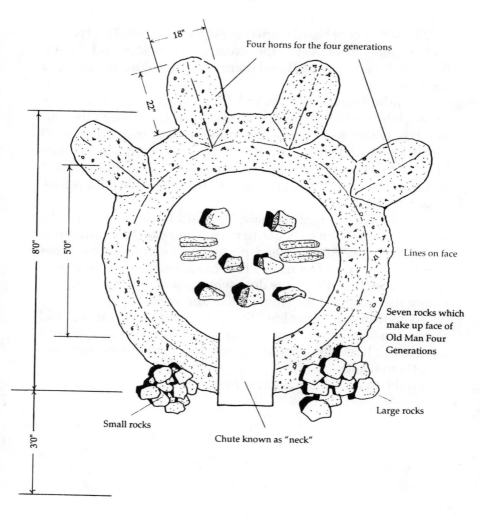

West
Λ

18"

22"

Four horns for the four generations

80"

50"

Lines on face

Seven rocks which make up face of Old Man Four Generations

Large rocks

30"

Small rocks

Chute known as "neck"

Lakota Old Man Four Generations sweat lodge

West
Λ

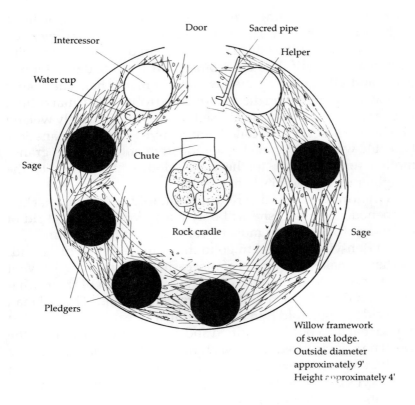

Intercessor

Door

Sacred pipe

Helper

Water cup

Sage

Chute

Rock cradle

Sage

Pledgers

Willow framework
of sweat lodge.
Outside diameter
approximately 9'
Height approximately 4'

Detailed plan of sweat lodge used for purification ceremony

Scar Face
(Blackfeet)

There was once a young man whose parents had died. He lived with his grandmother. The two of them were so poor they lived in an old lodge at the edge of the camp. In the same camp with them was a beautiful young woman. She was the daughter of a chief, and all the young men wanted to marry her. The young man whose parents had died also wanted to ask her to marry him, but he was too shy to do so himself. There was a big ugly welt on his cheek, and everyone called him Boh-yi-yi, which means Scar Face. He was afraid that she would laugh at him. So his grandmother agreed to go to the chief's lodge and speak to the daughter on Boh-yi-yi's behalf.

When his grandmother returned, she told Boh-yi-yi what had happened. "She says she will only marry you if you get rid of your scar. To do so you must travel to the land of the Sun."

So Boh-yi-yi decided to go to the Sun. He asked his grandmother to make many pairs of moccasins for him. Then he went to the wisest old men in the camp. He asked each of them what to do and then decided which one could help him. The old man he decided upon told him that they must sweat together all that day so that he would be purified and ready for his journey. In the sweat he was cleansed with sweetgrass and they smoked the pipe together. When the sweat was done, they ate the big meal which Boh-yi-yi's grandmother had prepared, and he gave the old man presents to thank him for his help.

Then Boh-yi-yi began to travel toward the land where the Sun lives. He carried sweetgrass and tobacco with him so that he could pray and ask for help along the way. He also carried a flint knife. He walked over the mountains and across the plains and he wore out one pair of moccasins after another. His feet became bloody and he was very weary. At last he came to a great wide lake and waded in to cool himself. Then he sat down by the lake and began to sing and pray. As he did so, a flock of swans came up to him.

"Why are you crying and praying with your feet in the water?" said the Swan Chief.

"I am trying to reach the place where Sun lives," Boh-yi-yi said, "but now I am tired and my feet are bleeding. I will not go back, so I have decided to die here."

Then the Swan Chief took pity on Boh-yi-yi. "My people know the trail to Sun's land," he said. "We will carry you there. Spread your robe and lie down on it and close your eyes."

Boh-yi-yi did as the Swan Chief told him. He spread his robe, lay down on it, and closed his eyes. As soon as he did so, he felt the robe lift him up into the air. The wind whistled around him and he fell asleep. When he opened his eyes, the swans were gone and he was on the shore of a lake which looked even bigger than the one where he met the swans.

Then he heard a cry. He looked up and saw a great bird, like a crane but much larger. It was chasing a young man and stabbing at him with its long beak. As he ran, the young man cried for help.

Boh-yi-yi leaped up and pulled out his flint knife. He ran at the great bird and stabbed it in the throat with his flint knife. The bird staggered and then fell. As he stood there, Boh-yi-yi realized that his feet no longer hurt. He looked down and saw a new pair of moccasins on his feet and realized that the swans must have given them to him and healed his blisters.

The young man came up and greeted Boh-yi-yi by grasping his hand. "O-ki," the young man said, "I greet you, brother. You are brave to face that terrible bird with only a knife. What is your name and why are you here?"

"I am Boh-yi-yi. I am trying to find the lodge of the Sun," Boh-yi-yi said.

"The Sun is my father," said the young man. "I am Morning Star. My father has gone for the night and will not be back until it is morning. But he always kills anyone who comes to his lodge. Let us go and talk to my mother. She may help you."

Morning Star led Boh-yi-yi to the lodge of the Sun. A beautiful woman with a lovely face sat there in front of the lodge. It was Morning Star's mother, the Moon.

"Mother," Morning Star said, "I have brought a friend here. He saved my life by killing the great crane. He has traveled far to come here and I want him to be my brother. Will you take pity on him?"

Moon looked at Boh-yi-yi and smiled. "You have saved the life of my son and you are welcome. Come inside," she said. "I will talk to my husband."

Boh-yi-yi followed Moon and Morning Star into the lodge. The floor of the lodge was covered with cedar boughs and there was a mound of earth in front of the door and an eagle wing fan. There dried cedar could be burned as a purifying smudge over a buffalo chips fire.

Moon and Morning Star seated Boh-yi-yi in the place of honor and gave him food. When he had finished eating, Moon said to him, "Why have you traveled so far? Is there something that you want from Sun?"

"Yes," Boh-yi-yi said, "I want to get rid of this scar on my face."

Now it was almost morning.

"It is time for me to leave," Morning Star said. "I must make one of my journeys as I do each day. Be brave and my father may help you." Then he left the lodge.

Soon Boh-yi-yi could feel things becoming warmer.

"My husband is coming," Moon said. Then she led Boh-yi-yi to the back of the lodge and covered him with cedar branches. As he lay there, it began to grow warmer and he moved about under the boughs.

"Be still," Moon whispered. "My husband is almost here."

It became hotter and hotter and Moon whispered, "Sun is at the door of the lodge."

Then a strong voice spoke. "Huh-ah-yah! Why does my lodge smell bad?"

"My husband," Moon said, "Morning Star brought a friend

to our lodge. He saved the life of our son from the great crane."

"Hah-you! Quick, burn some cedar and clean the air."

Moon burned cedar, and when the smoke had cleansed the air of the lodge, Sun came in. Boh-yi-yi felt the heat of Sun burning his body, even under the cedar boughs.

"Where is Morning Star's friend?" Sun said.

"We covered him with the cedar boughs," Moon said.

"Come out," Sun said.

Even though it was so hot that he could hardly breathe now, Boh-yi-yi stood up from under the cedar boughs. He did not look Sun in the face but kept his gaze down at the ground. Sun was pleased. He saw that this boy was unfortunate, but respectful. He made his heat grow less.

Before long, Morning Star returned from his journey and sat in his place in the lodge.

"My son," his father said, "do you want this young man for a friend?"

"Yes," Morning Star said. "I want him to be my brother. I want someone to travel with me on my journeys."

"Then you must make a sweat bath," said Sun.

Morning Star did as his father said. He prepared a sweat bath and then Sun went into it. He made everything ready inside and told the two young men to enter.

"Close the covers," he said to Moon, and she did as her husband asked. After a time, Sun called again to his wife, "Open the door."

When Moon lifted the cover and the light came into the sweat bath, she saw the two young men seated side by side. They now looked just alike.

"Which one is Morning Star?" Sun said.

"It is this one," said Moon.

"No," Sun said, "that is the one who was known as Boh-yi-yi. Now his name is Mistaken For Morning Star."

Now the two young men traveled together everywhere. Wherever Morning Star went, Boh-yi-yi was beside him. But at last the day came when Boh-yi-yi knew he must return to his people.

Sun spoke to him at great length. He gave him instructions on what he must do when he returned to the earth. He would marry that daughter of the chief, but he had a greater duty to perform. He must teach the people the way to honor the Sun and thank him for providing all the things that make life possible. He must teach them the way of the Sun Dance.

So Boh-yi-yi traveled back down to earth. He came floating down from the sky to the camp. As soon as he arrived, people rushed out to greet him, but he stopped them from coming close.

"You must prepare a sweat bath for me," he said. "Only after I have sweated can I tell you what I know."

So Boh-yi-yi sweated and when he came out of the sweat lodge he began to teach the people all that Sun had taught him. It took a long time to teach them, but Boh-yi-yi taught them well. They learned the way of the Sun Dance, a way which the people follow to this day.

As for Boh-yi-yi, he married the daughter of the chief and lived for a long time with the people. But the day finally came when he returned to the land of the Sun and his friend Morning Star. You may see the two friends together early in the morning and late at night as they journey together across the sky.

Weetucks Brings the Sweat
(Wampanoag)

Long ago, a boy was born in a village of the Land of First Light. His mother was a woman far past the age of childbearing, so the birth of this boy came as a great surprise. He was given the name Weetucks and it was said that his birth must have been meant as a special gift from the Creator.

As he grew, people noticed that this boy always listened closely to his elders and to everything said in council. Perhaps he would grow up to be a sachem or a pow-wow. Then, one day, Weetucks went to walk by the sea and did not return. His mother and the other people of the village searched for him, but no trace of the boy, Weetucks, could be found.

The sun rose and set many times, but Weetucks did not come home. Everyone in the village assumed that he was dead and his mother grieved for him. Then, when a full moon had passed, Weetucks returned. He came staggering into the village on the path which led from the water and fell down, half dead from fever, weak from hunger and exhaustion. As the people rushed to help him, they marveled at the fact that he was no longer a little boy but had grown to be a very large man.

The people carried him to the hut of his mother, wrapped him in warm skins beside the fire, and cared for him. Finally, after many sunrise and sunsets, his fever broke and he began to regain his strength.

"Bring the elders to me," Weetucks said. "I have things to teach them."

Soon the wisest elders of the village gathered in the wigwam. Then Weetucks began to explain to them the things which he had been taught while he was away in the land of the spirits. He taught them about the use of roots and berries and herbs for all kinds of medicine. He taught them the *pniese*, the ceremony which young boys must go through to pass into manhood, and he taught them the ceremony for young girls to prepare them to

121

be women. When he grew stronger, he left his bed and showed them how to make paint and how to draw pictures. He taught them how to use fire to hollow a log into a canoe, and how to make bows and arrows. There seemed no end to the things which Weetucks now knew and gave to the people.

Then Weetucks led the people to the edge of the water.

"Now," he said, "I will show you how to make a lodge which will give us strength and will cure us of many things.'

He laid stones in a circle to make the foundation of a hut and then finished it by bending saplings, tying them and covering them with mats made of rushes. He dug out the earth inside the lodge so that people could now step down into it and stand without touching the roof. Then he placed a platform of stones in the center of the lodge. On top of that bed of stones, he laid a fire and kept it burning until the stone were red with heat. Then he swept the remaining coals into a bark bucket and took them out of the lodge.

'It is ready now," he said. Then Weetucks called all of the people, men and women and children alike, to come into the lodge, one family at a time.

"This is how we will cleanse ourselves together," he said, closing the door so that no light could enter. He poured water on the hot stones and steam rose and filled the sweat bath, cleansing the people. They felt the heat enter their bodies, driving out sickness. They stayed in there, sitting or lying down, talking and sometimes singing together. When the stones had cooled, Weetucks opened the door and led the people to the water where they bathed and cooled themselves. Then another fire was laid to heat the stones once more for more people to be cleansed.

So the sweat bath was given to the Wampanoag people by Weetucks. He continued teaching the people until the day came when his own mother was called to the spirit land. Then he taught the people the last teaching. He taught them the Death Ceremonies, piling stones on his mother's grave and lighting a spirit fire.

At last, the time came for Weetucks to leave his people. He walked towards the bay and when he reached the water, he continued to walk on top of the waves. He walked until he was lost from sight in the sunset. But his teachings remained to strengthen the lives and the hearts of the people of the Land of First Light.

The Blanket of Men's Eyes
(Seneca)

There were two brothers who lived with their grandmother. They had a game which they often played together. One brother would go to the top of two small hills which were close to each other. He would jump from one hilltop to the next while his brother shot arrows at him from below.

In their grandmother's lodge an arrow hung. "Do not touch that arrow," their grandmother said. "It belonged to your father."

One day, though, when their grandmother was away, the boys took the arrow and went out to play their game. Older Brother went to the top of the two hills and as he leaped from one to the other, Younger Brother fired their father's arrow. But this arrow had special power. It flew straight toward Older Brother, struck him, and continued on, carrying him through the air.

Younger Brother was horrified. He ran as fast as he could, following the flight of the magic arrow as it carried his brother further and further to the north. He ran through most of the day and when the arrow fell at last, pinning Older Brother to the ground, the boys were further from their home than they had ever been.

"My brother," Younger Brother said, "I am sorry." He lifted his older brother up but was unable to remove the arrow.

"I am too weak to walk," Older Brother said. "You must carry me on your back. Follow this trail."

Carrying his wounded brother, the younger boy began to follow the trail.

"We must be careful as we follow this trail," said the wounded brother. "There is a lodge ahead of us where some dangerous people live. When you hear them singing and calling for us to join them, do not look towards them. If you look at them, you will die."

Now Younger Brother heard the sound of the women singing.

"Come and join us," the women called.

But Younger Brother kept his eyes on the trail and did not look up as he carried his wounded brother past them.

"We have gone past them," Older Brother said, "but there are more dangerous people ahead of us now. They are women who steal men's eyes with a magic blanket. The trail passes through their lodge and it is the only way we can go. We must not look at that magic blanket or we will be blinded."

The trail bent and there ahead of them it ran through a long lodge. Again Younger Brother kept his eyes on the ground as he walked into the lodge. he heard the voices of the women speaking from all sides.

"Look up at us."

"Why do you keep your eyes on the ground? Look at what we have here."

"Look at this beautiful blanket, see how the eyes on it wink at you."

No matter what they said, Younger Brother did not look up. But as he reached the end of the lodge, one of the women threw the blanket on the ground in front of him. Before he could close his own eyes, he saw the eyes on the blanket looking up at him. He saw the eyes on the blanket opening and closing and then his own eyes leaped from his head and he saw no more. He fell to his knees and felt his brother roll from his back.

"Brother," he called, "where are you?"

But his brother did not answer. All he heard were the women who owned the blanket of eyes.

"These new eyes are fine ones," they laughed. "They are different than any of our other eyes. See how red they are."

Younger Brother crawled forward on his knees, feeling his way with his hands. He left the long lodge behind him and crawled for a long time. At last he felt the edge of a field and stalks of corn and he curled up and slept.

When he woke, it was to the sound of a woman's voice singing. This song, though, was not like the songs he had heard from the dangerous women who stole men's eyes. This was a corn-harvesting song sung by a woman with a strong, sweet voice. The singing came closer and closer and then, suddenly, it stopped.

"Sister," the one who had been singing shouted, "come here. There is a man in our corn field." The blinded young man felt the hands of two women helping him to stand and leading him forward until he was brought into a lodge and seated by a fire.

"My older sister and I live alone here," said the woman who had been singing. "We wish to help you."

"I was carrying my brother on my back," Younger Brother said. "I had wounded him with an arrow. We came to the long lodge and there were women there with a blanket of men's eyes. They placed that blanket before my face and I became blind."

Gradually, with the care of the two sisters, Younger Brother regained his strength. Though blind, he was able to help the women with their work. One day, the older sister spoke to him.

"My younger sister, Beautiful Singer, and I are fond of you. You have been a good companion to us. You must marry her and remain with us as her husband."

Younger Brother agreed and Beautiful Singer became his wife. Several seasons passed and she gave birth to twin sons. They named them Hanonni-da, which means Thistle, and Hodada-o, which means Crier. Those boys grew very quickly, and it was obvious that they had special power. They began to talk soon after they were born and the first thing they asked for were lacrosse sticks and a ball so that they might play. Though they were babies, they played as well as grown men. Later they asked for bows and arrows and when they were given them, they began to hunt and bring back game.

One day, while their mother and aunt were out gathering berries in the forest, Hanonni-da and Hodada-o came and sat by their father.

"Father," they said, "why do you have no eyes?"

"I was traveling with my brother on my back, for I had wounded him with an arrow. When we passed through a long lodge, some dangerous women forced me to look upon a blanket made of men's eyes. That blanket stole my eyes and I lost my brother and was unable to find him."

"Father," said Hanonni-da, "we will find your lost brother for you."

"Father," said Hodada-o, "we will go to that long lodge and bring back your eyes."

"Do not try to do that," said Younger Brother. "Those dangerous women are too powerful. And my brother is surely dead. It has been many seasons since I lost him."

"Do not worry,' said Hanonni-da.

"We will go out and play now," said Hodada-o.

The boys left the lodge. However, they were not gone long when Younger Brother heard their voices again, first from far away as if under the ground and then from closer at hand.

"Do not let go of him," Hanonni-da said.

"Pull harder and soon we will reach where our father is waiting," said Hodada-o.

Then Younger Brother felt their hands guiding his hands.

"Grab hold, father," they said, as they placed his hands on the body of another human being. This person's clothing was tattered and he was very thin, but he was still alive. His face was thin, as if from hunger, and there were no eyes in his sockets. Then Younger Brother felt the arrow which was still lodged in the man's chest. It was Older Brother.

"Wait, father," the boys said, "we will borrow some eyes so that you can see our uncle."

The boys went out and took the eyes from a deer which they had just killed and brought back to the lodge for meat. They placed the eyes in Younger Brother's sockets. Now Younger Brother could see again, though it seemed as if he were looking through spider webs. His older brother lay on the floor in front of him, almost as thin as a skeleton.

"Our uncle will become well after he has eaten," said Hanonni-da.

"Those eyes we have borrowed from the deer will not last long, father," said Hodada-o. "But we will soon get your own eyes back."

Then the two boys left the lodge and went toward the place where their father and uncle had lost their eyes. As they walked, they made their plan. There was a spring near the long lodge where the dangerous women lived. Each day the women went there to get water.

Hanonni-da hid himself in the bushes near the spring and Hodada-o changed himself into a small duck. As soon as one of the women came down to get water, she saw the duck, but when she tried to grab it, the duck which was Hodada-o entered her body. When that woman got back to the long lodge, the eldest of the women there looked closely at her.

"Daughter," the old woman said, "it appears that you are about to have a child."

Even as she said those words, the younger woman began to gave birth. She gave birth to a baby boy. All the woman gathered around to look at this marvelous baby, who was actually Hodada-o. He was a beautiful child, but he would not stop crying. Nothing the woman did would stop his cries.

"Try singing to him."

"Rock him in your arms."

"Put him in this cradleboard."

At last they decided he needed something to play with. The old woman looked around the lodge and saw their magical blanket of men's eyes. She brought it over.

"Perhaps he would like to play with our magic blanket," she said. As soon as she placed the blanket over Hodada-o he stopped crying and seemed to fall asleep. The women then quietly left the lodge so that he would not waken. As soon as they were gone. Hodada-o resumed his own shape, folded the blanket up, and ran out of the lodge with it.

The women saw him as he came out.

"He has stolen our blanket," they cried and they began to

pursue him. They dropped the shapes of women which they had taken and took their own shapes, which were the shapes of monsters. They had clubs in their hands and struck at Hodada-o with them, but he was too quick for them. He ran in and out among them, ducking and dodging so that each time one of the women struck at him and missed, she hit and killed her own sister. He ran in between the last two and they struck each other with their clubs. Now all of those who had stolen men's eyes were dead.

Hodada-o joined his brother Hanonni-da, who now had a large bundle on his back. Together they brought the magic blanket back to the lodge where their father and uncle waited.

"Father," they said, "which of these eyes are yours?"

"You will recognize them easily," he said, "They have a reddish color."

They picked out their father's eyes from the magic blanket and gave them to him and his sight was restored. They also found the eyes of Older Brother and gave them back to him. Then they made a small sweat lodge and covered it with the skin of a white bear and placed their father's brother inside. When they uncovered the lodge, the arrow had fallen from his chest and he was whole and strong again.

"There are others who died when they were blinded," said Older Brother. "Their eyes are still part of the magic blanket."

"We will help them, too, Uncle," said Hanonni-da, placing the bundle he had carried from the long lodge on the ground and opening it to show that it was filled with many human bones. "I have gathered all of them here."

Then Hanonni-da and Hodada-o placed the bones and the blanket of men's eyes in the sweat lodge and covered it with the white bear skin a second time. Before long, the lodge began to shake and quiver. Then Hodada-o went over to a large hickory tree and leaned hard on it.

"Jump up quickly," he shouted. "A tree is about to fall on the sweat lodge."

The Blanket of Men's Eyes 129

Then all of the bones in the sweat lodge came back together. Flesh came back onto the bones and the eyes from the blanket went back into the sockets of the men who had lost them. Alive and well, all of those people jumped out of the sweat lodge.

Older Brother and Younger Brother made a village there for all of those people. Older Brother married the older sister of Beautiful Singer and, with the wonderful twins Hanonni-da and Hodada-o to help them, all of those people lived together happily. So the story ends.

Turtle Man
(Cheyenne)

Long ago, there were two brothers. The older brother was married. He was jealous of his younger brother, whose name was Spotted Hawk. Spotted Hawk was not married. He lived with the older brother and his wife in a lodge set up some distance from the main camp. One day, the older brother walked by the river and saw a tall, dead tree leaning out on a bluff high over the water. He went back to his lodge and sat and thought for a while. Then he called his younger brother to him.

"I saw an eagle's nest in a tree by the river, but I am not a good climber. Come with me and climb up to the nest so we can get their feathers."

When they reached the tree, Spotted Hawk began to climb. When he reached the top of the tree, he saw the nest was old and long deserted. But as he looked down to call out that the eagles were gone, he saw his brother pushing against the tree. The tree began to lean further and further. Then it fell off the bluff into the swift waters of the river and Spotted Hawk was drowned.

The older brother went back to the lodge and pretended to be in great distress. "Enemies attacked us," he said to his wife. "Spotted Hawk was killed and they carried away his body. We must move our lodge back to the main camp."

When they reached the camp, he told his mother the story of Spotted Hawk's death. All the people in the camp grieved, for everyone had liked Spotted Hawk.

Down river from the place where Spotted Hawk drowned there lived an underwater person and his daughter. One day, as the daughter swam in the river, she saw the body of a young man washed up on the sand. She went to tell her father.

"Aho," the father said, "I must go and get that young man. I think I can cure him. I will make a sweat lodge for him and when he is better he can be your husband."

Then the father went to the place where Spotted Hawk's body

lay. The old underwater man dragged Spotted Hawk out of the river. The young man's body was all covered with sand, but the old underwater man carried him up the bank. There he made a fire to heat stones and he built a sweat lodge out of willow poles, covering it with a buffalo skin. He poured water on the stones and sang over Spotted Hawk's body. Some of the sand fell off, but when he was done, Spotted Hawk was still dead.

The old underwater man made a second sweat lodge and sang over Spotted Hawk again. Again more sand fell off, but Spotted Hawk was not yet alive. The old underwater man made a third sweat lodge and then a fourth one. When he had finished singing over Spotted Hawk in the fourth sweat lodge, all of the sand was gone from the young man's body. When that sweat ended, Spotted Hawk sat up and opened his eyes. The old underwater man had cured him.

The father brought Spotted Hawk back to their lodge by the river and told his daughter, "Bring some food for our guest. See what kind of food he likes to eat."

The daughter went out and came back with a bowl full of leeches.

"I cannot eat that food," Spotted Hawk said.

"Go and gather greens for him," the father said. The daughter went out and came back with the bowl filled with river weeds.

"I cannot eat that food," Spotted Hawk said.

"Ask him what kind of food he does eat," said the father.

"What food can we bring you that you like to eat?" the daughter asked.

"I like to eat buffalo meat," said Spotted Hawk. "That is my food."

Then the daughter went out and came back with buffalo meat, but the meat was raw.

"I cannot eat that until it has been cooked," said Spotted Hawk.

So the father made a fire and the buffalo meat was cooked for Spotted Hawk, who ate it and was content.

The father and the daughter were kind to Spotted Hawk and he enjoyed living with them. He and the daughter married and set up a lodge of their own next to his father-in-law's. Soon they had a child, a little boy who grew quickly. Spotted Hawk loved his new family very much, but he began to think about his mother. One day, as Spotted Hawk was out hunting near the river, he saw an old woman standing on a hilltop. She looked familiar and when he crept close to her he saw that it was his own mother. He stood so that she could see him.

"My son," she cried out, "are you alive?"

Spotted Hawk embraced his mother and told her what had happened to him, how his brother had pushed the dead tree into the water, and how the old man had saved him.

"You must meet my wife and our son," Spotted Hawk said.

"First come back with me to our camp," his mother said. "All our relatives will be glad to see you."

So Spotted Hawk went with his mother back to the camp. His older brother saw Spotted Hawk coming and left the camp in shame. He was never seen again. But the people rejoiced to have Spotted Hawk back with them. They made food for him and there was celebration.

"Stay with us," the people said, but Spotted Hawk was eager to return to his wife and their son.

"I will go with you," said Spotted Hawk's mother, "I want to see my grandson."

So Spotted Hawk and his mother set out across the prairie for the place by the river where Spotted Hawk had been living with his father-in-law, his wife, and their son. From the top of a hill, they saw two lodges standing close to the river's edge. But as they came close, the lodges became smaller and smaller until they vanished. Where the lodges had been, all that Spotted Hawk and his mother saw were two large turtles and one small one. The three turtles went toward the river as quickly as they could and sank under the water.

Spotted Hawk was filled with sorrow. He had lost his wife

and their son.

"Leave me here by the river," he said to his mother. Alone with his grief, Spotted Hawk sat by the river for three days. He did not eat or sleep, all that he did was mourn and cry for his lost family. Then, on the morning of the fourth day, the head of a small turtle came up in the water close to him.

"Father," the small turtle said, "you must try to catch me. Mother is trying to persuade grandfather to allow you to return to us. But if you don't catch me and hold on to me, we will never be together again."

Spotted Hawk dove into the river, but the small turtle had already swum away beneath the surface. So Spotted Hawk waited there by the river. Each day the small turtle came back and each day Spotted Hawk tried in vain to catch his son. Finally, on the fourth day, Spotted Hawk almost grabbed hold of the small turtle before it sank beneath the surface. Spotted Hawk dove after it. He could barely see it beneath the water as it went down deeper and deeper. Spotted Hawk thought he would drown, but he did not give up. He swam down and down after it and just barely grasped it with his fingertips. He came out of the water holding the small turtle close to his chest.

"I will not let you go, my son," Spotted Hawk said. The little turtle did not answer him, but Spotted Hawk did not let go. He stayed there for four days, holding the little turtle. On the fourth day, the little turtle spoke.

"Father," he said, "mother has now convinced grandfather to allow you to return to us. Carry me down to the water and hold on to my tail and I will take you back to our family."

Spotted Hawk did as his son told him. He placed the small turtle in the deep water and held on to his tail. Then the little turtle began to swim, pulling Spotted Hawk after him. They went down and down until they came to a hole in the cliff under the water. They passed through that hole and came out into a place where there were many lodges of the underwater people. Now Spotted Hawk's son no longer looked like a turtle, but stood beside his father. And there before them was Spotted Hawk's wife, holding out her arms to them.

Spotted Hawk and his wife and son all lived there together for a long time and they were happy. One day, Spotted Hawk asked his son if he could go and visit his human relatives. It was the time of year when the Cheyenne would follow the buffalo to the place near the river and he knew he could find their camp.

"Since you have asked, father," said his son, "you may go and visit them and you are free to return to us."

When Spotted Hawk came into the camp, his mother and all the other people were very glad to see him.

"My name is no longer Spotted Hawk," he said. "I am Turtle Man now. And I have come back to give you something that will bring good to the people."

Then Turtle Man built a sweat lodge for the people. He showed them how to use it, for they had never seen a sweat lodge before. It was in the shape of a turtle, in honor of the underwater people who had brought him back to life and taught him about it. Ever since then, thanks to Turtle Man, the Cheyenne people have had the sweat lodge.

Walking in November Across the Stream to the Sweat Lodge

In memory of Sam Ray

The leaves fallen
from the creekside maples,
no longer blaze as red as embers.

Earth brown, they close
like fists around
their own lives,
loosening into soil.

My red dog grabs a stick in her mouth,
so long it knocks against the trees
as she runs up the narrow path,
making a music which startles, delights her.

No great issues this morning,
no more to do than burn tobacco,
speak words by the fire pit,
strip the blankets from the sweat lodge.

One old quilt has become as thin as paper.
I laugh as I lift it—the white-footed mice
have stolen the batting to weave into nests.
Light shines through its patterns
of red and orange, a sudden flower.

Walking back, the wind against my face,
I am suddenly wreathed in clouds of breath.

There is no way to count
the blessings of seasons,
the fallen leaves.

Further Reading

In writing this book I have not focused on direct descriptions of the building of sweat lodges and the exact ceremonial uses of sweats by specific Native peoples. Such descriptions can be found in many places, most frequently of the Lakota inipi. Here are a few good examples:

Imagine Ourselves Richly: Mythic Narratives of North American Indians: Chapter 7, "The Genesis of Phillip Deere's Sweat Lodge." (Creek)

Lame Deer, Seeker of Visions: Chapter 10, "Inipi—Grandfather's Breath." (Lakota)

The Mishomis Book: Chapter 12, "The Sweat Lodge." (Anishinabe)

The Sacred Pipe: Black Elk's Account of the Seven Rites of the Oglala Sioux: Chapter III, "Inipi, The Rite of Purification." (Lakota)

Sweat: Chapter 6, "The Native American Sweat Lodge." (Lakota and Dineh, also Mexican temescal)

Bibliography

Aaland, Mikkel. *Sweat*. Santa Barbara: Capra Press, 1978.

Amiotte, Arthur, "Eagles Fly Over," in *Parabola*, Volume 1, Number 3, Summer 1976.

Beck, Peggy V.; Walters, Anna Lee; and Francisco, Nia. *The Sacred: Ways of Knowledge, Sources of Life*. Tsaile, AZ: Navajo Community College Press, 1977 (second edition, 1992).

Benton Benai, Edward. *The Mishomis Book: The Voice of the Ojibway*. St. Paul, MN: Indian Country Press, 1979.

Brown, Joseph Epes. *The Sacred Pipe: Black Elk's Account of the Seven Rites of the Oglala Sioux*. Norman: University of Oklahoma, 1953.

Bullchild, Percy. *The Sun Came Down: The History of the World as My Blackfeet Elders Told It*. New York: Harper and Row, 1985.

Clark, Ella E. *Indian Legends of the Pacific Northwest*. Berkeley: University of California Press, 1953.

————. *Indian Legends from the Northern Rockies*. Norman: University of Oklahoma, 1966.

Churchill, Ward. *Fantasies of the Master Race: Literature, Cinema and the Colonization of American Indians*. Monroe, ME: Common Courage Press, 1992.

Coe, Michael D. *The Maya*. New York: Praeger Publishing, 1977.

Deloria, Ella, *Dakota Texts*. Vermillion: Dakota Press, 1978.

Eargle, Dolan H. Jr. *The Earth is Our Mother: A Guide to the Indians of California, Their Locales and Historic Sites*. San Francisco: Trees Company Press, 1986.

Eastman, Charles A. *The Soul of the Indian*. Boston: Houghton Mifflin, 1911.

Erdoes, Richard. *Crying for a Dream*. Santa Fe: Bear & Co., 1990.

Gilmore, Melvin R. *Prairie Smoke*. St. Paul: Minnesota Historical Society Press, 1987.

Grinell, George Bird. *By Cheyenne Campfires*. New Haven: Yale University Press, 1926.

―――. *The Punishment of the Stingy and Other Indian Stories*. New York: Harper and Brothers, 1901.

Heizer, Robert F., and Elsasser, Albert. *The Natural World of the California Indians*. Berkeley: University of California Press, 1980.

Hines, Doland A. *Ghost Voices: Yakima Indian Myths, Legends, Humor and Hunting Stories*. Great Issaquah, WA: Eagle Publishing, 1992.

Horse Capture, George, ed. *The Seven Visions of Bull Lodge*. Lincoln: University of Nebraska, 1980.

Jamimes, M. Annette, ed. *The State of Native America*. Boston: South End Press, 1992.

Kluckhohn, Clyde and Leighton, Dorothea. *The Navaho*. Cambridge: Harvard University Press, 1974.

Lame Deer, John, and Erdoes, Richard. *Lame Deer, Seeker of Visions*. Englewood Cliffs, NJ: Simon & Schuster, 1972.

Laubin, Reginald, and Laubin, Gladys. *The Indian Tipi*. Norman: University of Oklahoma Press, 1977.

Leland, Charles G. *The Algonquin Legends of New England*. Boston: Houghton Mifflin, 1884.

Lewis, Oscar. *Tepoztitlan: Village in Mexico*. New York: Holt Rinehart Winston, 1960.

Linderman, Frank B. *Plenty Coups, Chief of the Crows.* Lincoln: University of Nebraska Press, 1962.

Lopatin, Ivan A. "Origin of the Native American Sweat Bath," *American Anthropologist* 62: 977–993, 1960.

Luckert, Karl W. *The Navajo Hunter Tradition.* Tucson: University of Arizona Press, 1975.

Malotki, Ekkehart, and Lomatuway'ma, Michael. *Hopi Coyote Tales* Lincoln: University of Nebraska Press, 1984.

Masson, Marcelle. *A Bag of Bones: Legends of the Wintu Indians of Northern California.* Happy Camp, CA: Naturegraph, 1966.

Oakes, Maud. *The Two Crosses of Todos Santos.* Princeton, NJ: Princeton University Press, 1951.

Parker, Arthur C. *Seneca Myths and Folk Tales.* Buffalo, NY: Buffalo Historical Society, 1923.

Quintasket, Christine (Mourning Dove). *Coyote Stories.* Lincoln: University of Nebraska Press, 1990.

Ramsey, Jarold. *Coyote Was Going There: Indian Literature of the Oregon Country.* Seattle: University of Washington Press, 1977.

———. *Reading The Fire: Essays in the Traditional Indian Literatures of the West.* Lincoln: University of Nebraska, 1983.

Rockwell, David. *Giving Voice to Bear: North American Indian Myths, Rituals and Images of the Bear.* Niwot, CO: Roberts Rinehart, 1991.

Russell, Howard S. *Indian New England Before the Mayflower.* Hanover, NH: University Press of New England, 1980.

Tantaquidgeon, Gladys. *Folk Medicine of the Delaware.* Marrisburg, PA: Pennsylvania Historical and Museum Commission Anthropological Series No. 3, 1972.

Tedlock, Barbara, and Tedlock, Dennis. *Teachings from the American Earth: Indian Religion and Philosophy.* New York: Liveright, 1975.

Thwaites, Reuben Gold, ed. *Travels and Explorations of the Jesuit Missionaries in New France 1610-1791.* Cleveland: The Burrows Brothers, 1899.

Tooker, Elizabeth. *An Ethnography of the Huron Indians, 1615–1649.* Syracuse: Syracuse University Press, 1991

Vaudrin, Bill. *Tanaina Tales from Alaska.* Norman: University of Oklahoma Press, 1969.

Vecsey, Christopher. *Imagine Ourselves Richly: Mythic Narratives of North American Indians.* New York: Harper Collins, 1991.

Vogel, Virgil J. *American Indian Medicine.* New York: Ballantine Books, 1973.

Vogt, Evon Z. *The Zinacantecos of Mexico: A Modern Maya Way of Life.* New York: Holt Rinehart Winston, 1970.

Walker, James R. *Lakota Myth.* Lincoln: University of Nebraska Press, 1983.

Weil, Andrew. "The Indian Sweat," *American West,* 19: 42–49, 1982.

Weslager, C.A. *The Delaware Indians: A History.* New Brunswick, NJ: Rutgers University Press, 1972.

Wherry, Joseph H. *Indian Masks and Myths of the West.* New York: Apollo Editions, 1974.

Whiting, A. F. (edited by Steven A. Weber and P. Donald Seaman). *Havasupai Habitat.* Tucson: University of Arizona Press, 1985.

Wissler, Clark. *Star Legends Among the American Indians.* New York: American Museum of Natural History Science Guide No. 91, 1952.

Yazzie, Ethelou, ed. *Navajo History*. Chinle: Rough Rock Press, 1971.

Zolbrod, Paul. *Dine' bahane': The Navajo Creation Story*. Albuquerque: University of New Mexico Press, 1984.

The Crossing Press
publishes a full selection of titles
of general interest.
To receive our current catalog,
please call, Toll Free,
800/777-1048.